Most film distributors keep the secrets of their trade to themselves. While there are many books on the glamorous and technical aspects of motion picture production, few exist which deal extensively with the distribution practice.

This much needed volume serves as a long-awaited introduction to motion picture distribution. At last producers and their backers can learn about this vital topic, theory and practice; can read a variety of contracts between distributors and sub-distributors; distributors and exhibitors, etc. At last, movie personnel, trying to educate young assistants and secretaries, can furnish them with a fascinating easy-to-read guide.

The Don Rico illustrations of rackets may educate both potential victims and potential racketeers.

There has long been an increasing demand for books concerning motion picture distribution. This work helps fill the need.

> Michael B. Druxman,
> Hollywood publicist, film
> historian, and author, of
> *Paul Muni: His Life and His Films,*
> as well as other books and articles.

OTHER BOOKS BY THE AUTHOR(S):

The Record Industry Book

The Music Industry Book

The Publisher's Office Manual

The U.S. Master Producers & British Music Scene Book

The Movie Industry Book

The Managers, Entertainers & Agents Book

Film/TV Law (Your Introduction To Film/TV
    Copyright, Contracts & Other Law)

Film Superlist: 20,000 Motion Pictures In The
    United States Public Domain

Music/Record Business & Law (Your Introduction To
    Music/Record Copyright, Contracts & Other
    Business & Law)

Motion Picture Distribution (Business &/Or Racket?)

POSTER

The Entertainment Industry Money Flow Chart

DEDICATION

This book is dedicated to the men and women whose brains I picked when they were kind enough to contribute forms or to deliver guest lectures to my class on "Production Management and Packaging" at Columbia College.

Al Bergman

Richard Bernstein

Tony Cardoza

Jaacov Jaacovi

Natalie Jacobs

Marvin Miller

Don Rico

David Sheldon

Leseur Stewart

Andre Stojka

Paul Sylbert

Les Taxes

Mark Tenzer

Calvin Ward

Joy Wilkerson

MOTION PICTURE DISTRIBUTION

(BUSINESS AND/OR RACKET?!?)

BY

WALTER E. HURST

AND

WM. STORM HALE

AUTHORS OF
"FILM-TV LAW," "THE MOVIE INDUSTRY
BOOK" AND OTHER BOOKS IN
THE ENTERTAINMENT INDUSTRY "SERIES
••••

7 ARTS PRESS, INC.

Foreword by Michael B. Druxman
Introduction by Marvin Miller
Cover and Illustrations by Donato Rico
Typography by M. Anderson

MOTION PICTURE DISTRIBUTION, BUSINESS +/OR RACKET?!?

© Copyright 1975 by Walter E. Hurst
All Rights Reserved, International Copyright Secured
Manufactured in the U.S.A.

Library of Congress Cataloging in Publication Data

Hurst, Walter E
    Motion picture distribution (business and/or racket?!?).

    (Entertainment industry series ; v. 10)
    1. Moving-picture industry--United States.
2. Moving-pictures--Distribution. I. Title.
II. Series.
PN1993.5.U6H86   338.4'7'791430973   74-31299
ISBN 0-911370-23-4
ISBN 0-911370-24-2 pbk.

This is Volume 10 of The Entertainment Industry Series.
U.S. ISSN 0071–0695
For additional copies of this book, mail $10.00 in cash, check or money order to:
SEVEN ARTS PRESS, INC.
6605 Hollywood Boulevard, No. 215
Hollywood, CA 90028

iv

INTRODUCTION

When I completed my first picture, MAN AND WIFE, I felt like a mere babe-in-the-woods compared to the knowledgeable in-fighters in the motion picture distribution business. Since them I have learned about motion picture distribution, both in its business aspects and its unfortunate unethical and illegal practices, (which practices are cleverly illustrated in this book by Don Rico). I have learned the hard way, by trial and error, many of the lessons concerning distribution which are contained in this book. I wish I had known the information in this book before I entered distribution; I could have recognized and better exploited opportunities; I could have recognized and better avoided sharpsters' traps. This book will help readers in motion picture distribution, and those who want to be.

— Marvin Miller

Hollywood, California

TABLE OF CONTENTS

CHAPTERS

WALTER E. HURST

CHAPTER 1

ADVERTISING

"**Paid advertising** includes all newsprint, radio and television spots, billboards . . .

"**Publicity** involves obtaining 'free advertising' for a film via newspaper, magazine, radio and television editorial space, feature stories, interviews, column blurbs, etc. . . .

"**Exploitation** generally refers to exploiting a specific aspect of a movie for publicity purposes (and to generate word-of-mouth) by using gimmicks, stunts, and other attention getting devices.

"**Promotion** usually involves a commercial tie-in between a film and a product and/or personality."

THOSE GREAT MOVIE ADS.
Morella, Epstein, Clark.

Those GREAT MOVIE ADS contains lots of buff stuff, and an informative professional article, "A Brief Look at Movie Advertising." Sub-headings of the professional article include: Market Research; Contractural Obligations; Censorship; Radio-TV Spots; New "Art Film" Movement; Up There — Dow There Campaigns; Creative Excerpting; Publicity; Exploitation/Promotion; In-House Vs Agency; Coming Attractions; Teaser Ads; Awards. We very strongly recommend that the entire article be read and studied.

The book contains hundreds of advertisements and chapter headings include: Introduction, by Judith Crist; Critics' Quotes, Gimmee the Schmeer, Logos, Movies From Other Media, Comic Strip Features, Great Ad Lines, Together Again, A Brief Look At Movie Advertising, The Director As Star, Sequels and Series, Music and the Movies, Misleading Ad Lines, Selling the Trade, The Evolution of a Movie Ad, From a Movie Ad Man's Desk.

Additional chapters are: Gone With The Wind, Selling Technical Changes, Throwaways, Stars, "Go see it," Says Your

Favorite Star, Tie-Ins and Endorsements, Films From Other Lands, Special Situations, Classics, Censorship and Advertising, Let's Make It Again, Walt Disney, Fan Magazines, Fan Quiz, Press Books, Turnaround Campaigns.

There is so much contained in THOSE GREAT MOVIE ADS for readers seriously interested in motion picture distribution, that we strongly recommend you acquire your own copy from Galahad Books, New York City. The book is a "remainder," and the copy we acquired was listed as $14.95 reduced to $6.95.

Theories concerning ads vary. One theory is that ads should instruct the reader truthfully: if the movie is a comedy, the ad should be funny; if the movie is a Western, show the costumed man and appropriate animals; if the movie is the motorcycle violence type, show motorcycles and riders and their violence, etc.

Ads are usually prepared at the behest of distributors; they are prepared in various sizes (height, width); ads, plugs, stories, reviews are reproduced in press books; press books are sent to exhibitors; exhibitors select the appropriate size of ad; exhibitors send appropriate ads, plugs, reviews to local newspapers; sometimes the just mentioned tasks of the exhibitor are performed by the sub-distributor, national distributor, or local exchange personnel.

Who pays for the ads. That depends upon agreement between the exhibitor and the sub-distributor. A chain may be powerful enough to force the sub-distributor to pay the full amount of estimated advertising cost to the chain weeks before the playdates. The exhibitor chain does not want the newspapers burned by the sub-distributor's failure to pay the local newspapers. The chain does not wish to take a chance on the newspapers not carrying the necessary advertisements before and while the pictures are playing.

The sub-distributor in turn, utilizes not his own money, but that of the distributor. The sub-distributor utilizes money that he received from exhibitors for previous pictures. This utilizing money earned from previous pictures to pay for advertising later pictures, is one reason why sub-distributors are so slow in paying distributors for previous pictures.

If the later pictures should bomb, so that the sub-distributor does not rate any pay from the exhibitor in connection with the playing of the later pictures, the sub-distributor is in trouble. He no longer can pay the money he used for advertising the later pictures to the distributor of the earlier picture.

This, in turn, causes loss of income to the producers of the earlier picture.

Thus a bomb may hurt not only the producer of the bomb by never generating any money for him. The bomb can also hurt the producer of other pictures, as well as the bomb's distributor and sub-distributor.

CHAPTER 2

AUDITING BOX OFFICES . . .
AND TO SUE OR NOT TO SUE.

PRODUCERS vs. DISTRIBUTORS
DISTRIBUTORS vs. SUB-DISTRIBUTORS
SUB-DISTRIBUTORS vs. EXHIBITORS

Generally, a lawsuit is a horribly time-consuming and expensive procedure. It is a remedy that is sometimes worse than the disease.

Producers (know, believe, know and believe) that they are being cheated by distributors, sub-distributors and exhibitors. Distributors (know, believe, know and believe) that they are being cheated by sub-distributors and exhibitors. Sub-distributors (know, believe, know and believe) that they are being cheated by exhibitors.

One way to turn belief into knowledge, and to turn knowledge into proof, is to audit.

The right to audit should be placed into the contracts: the producer-distributor contract; the distributor-sub contract; the distributor-exhibitor contract; the exhibitor-sub contract.

The contractual right to audit could go one step further. The producer could insist that the distributor appoint a stipulated person to audit the sub-distributors and the exhibitors, and that such person provide information to both the producer and the distributor.

Rather than have just one person, one auditor, travel around the country auditing books, it might be better to have one firm of accountants in each city in which an exchange or a sub-distributor is located.

This would have several advantages.

Accountants charge for time; whether they openly list the charge or not, accountants are aware that they must consider their travel time when computing their bill. By reducing travel time, bills are reduced to that time period during which the accountant is actively working on the job.

If possible, one firm of accountants in each exchange city

should be used by many producers and distributors. This would enable the accountants to specialize in their field, to spend maximum time efficiently studying books and records. After the selected accountants have digested books and articles and the distribution business, the accountants will be able to apply their accounting knowledge to the books and records of the audited parties. Informational books include MOTION PICTURE DISTRIBUTION (Business Or Racket?).

Once an accountant has audited the books and records of a sub-distributor for Distributor No. 1, the accountant can easily audit the books for Distributor No. 2.

In fact, if the accountant represents Distributors 1, 2, 3, 4, and 5, then he can audit the sub-distributor at one session for the five distributors. The accountant will be able to do a better job at finding places where the sub-distributor deducts the same freight bill or advertising expense from more than one distributor.

In the music industry, many music publishers belong to *one service* which causes audits to be made of many record companies.

In the movie industry, there is a need for a service which will cause audits to be made of many distributors, sub-distributors and exhibitors.

This service could be called the Motion Picture Information Service. (MPIS)

The MPIS could be funded by a 1% contribution of gross receipts by the sub-distributor, a 1% contribution of gross receipts by the distributor, a 1% contribution of gross receipts by the producer. The contracts between the parties would have to provide that no party can pass that expense along to any party down the line (i.e., the sub can't deduct his 1% dues from the distributor).

The Motion Picture Information Service, in turn, would employ local accountants to perform the auditing functions. These accountants must not be persons who have as clients any exhibitors, subs, distributors or producers. This would be important to avoid conflict of interest and even the appearance of conflict of interest.

The MPIS could have a committee which could establish recommended uniform forms and bookkeeping to simplify auditing, make cheating more difficult, and to enter the information into computers.

One important consideration of potential accountants selected by MPIS is the accountant's potential appearance in court. The accountant should be interviewed concerning his willingness to testify in court. (Many personal injury cases have been settled for a sum unjust to the injured victim because the victim's doctor refused to testify in court). The accountant's appearance of credibility on direct examination and cross-examination should be checked into. (Many honest people can't express themselves, make clear their findings, and just don't give the appearance of honesty.)

The second member of the auditor-lawyer team is the lawyer.

Lawyers tend to specialize in one or more fields of law, and to avoid other fields of law.

The lawyers who are selected to sue crooked distributors, subs, and exhibitors should have experience in the fields of (a) trial law, (b) collecting, (c) accounting. The selected lawyers can quickly pick up information about the distribution business from MOTION PICTURE DISTRIBUTION (Business or Racket?). There are ample legal cases concerning illegal distribution practices in law books.

Conflict of interest should be avoided in that no lawyer should be selected to sue a client or former client. However, a lawyer who represents exhibitors or subs or distributors other than the one being sued, might be a very good lawyer for the case at hand because of his general knowledge of the industry.

One of the services of the Motion Picture Information Service could be the publication of information in magazine or newsletter form. MPIS could publish a looseleaf book directed at accountants, and a looseleaf book directed at attorneys.

The book for attorneys could contain sample complaints (the initial pleading in an action), sample interrogatories (the written questions which can be sent to the defendant to make him admit his actions and figures), sample summations to the judge or jury, and other sample pleadings.

Some lawyers in the pornography field have shared sample pleadings for years, with good results for their clients.

Such sample pleading enable attorneys to do their work more efficiently and with less time.

The use of laymen to practice licensed professions such as law and accounting by having laymen work for licensed lawyers and accountants has worked fairly well.

The layman is called para-legal or para-medical.

When the para-legal layman does the same work over and over again, while his employer-lawyer does a variety of work, the layman may be able to do this work more efficiently than the lawyer.

Collection agency lawyers have used para-legal assistants and legal secretaries for years. Often the collection agency attorney merely signs his name to the legal pleading and appears in court — all investigation, preparation of pleadings (filling in blank spaces on pre-printed forms), negotiation with the defendant, is done by para-legal assistants. This enables the attorney and his staff to render quality service for relatively low fees.

The same combination of licensed professionals and their unlicensed assistants might work in this field of attempting to collect from distributors, subs, and exchanges.

The more the work is done by para-professionals, the more the work is made routine and standard, the less time need be spent by the professionals, and the lower will be the fees.

There are several reasons for not suing, and there are points to be made concerning each reason.

1. **Reason for not suing.** Suing is slow. If a defendant is sued, he may not pay out of stubborness. **Point.** Big deal. The villain will always have a reason to not pay. Before he was sued, the reason he did not pay was because he was not sued.

2. **Reason for not suing.** Suing is slow. It takes years to get to court. **Point.** The villain may pay faster to avoid having to pay legal fees to his attorney (and if the contract so provides, paying for plaintiff's attorney).

3. **Reason for not suing.** The lawsuit takes up the time of the plaintiff, time the plaintiff could spend in other ways. **Point.** The injured party is in business; lawsuits are a tool to help him; if the businessman is too lazy to help himself and the people who depend on him, he is a prime pigeon for the villain who cheats him.

4. **Reason for not suing.** The producer is so broke, he can't afford to sue. His income from driving a cab is hardly

enough to pay his alimony. **Point.** That's a prime reason for setting up the system discussed herein, so that he need not come up with money in front.

The system as outlined here includes:

1. The Motion Picture Information Service, a fact-gathering, computer-using, information distributing service, which causes audits of money owers (exhibitors, subs, distributors) and supplies information to rightful money recipients (producers, distributors, subs).

2. Independent accountants in each exchange area. The question of whether they should be certified public accountants or not needs discussion. One firm should be selected in each area.

3. Independent attorneys in each exchange area. As few firms as possible, to enable specialization, should be selected in each area.

4. The project should be funded by a gross receipts fee applied on the gross receipts of each member of the Motion Picture Information Service. An alternative funding method, such as a membership fee, may be considered.

5. The preparation of uniform systems and forms to be used by all parties reporting income to other parties.

6. The preparation of litigations aids to attorneys to help achieve maximum efficiency at minimum expense to the clients.

LEGAL TACTICS AGAINST SUSPECTED CHEATERS

The deadbeat exhibitors, subs and distributors who cheat have three favorite tactics to discourage their victims from suing them:

Tactic One: threatening bankruptcy.

Tactic Two: having the corporation which owns the business go bankrupt.

Tactic Three: having the individual who owns the business or the stock of the corporation go bankrupt.

The plaintiff who is thinking of suing the deadbeat should discuss with his attorney:

1. suing not only for breach of contract, but also for wilful and malicious fraud before executing the contract, in rendering fraudulent statements, and in his whole scheme of doing business. A judgment might be for (1) the amount due to the plaintiff and (2) an extra amount awarded as punitive damages. Also, the defendant might not be able to wipe out such an award by going bankrupt; the award might survive the bankruptcy.

2. suing not only the corporation, but also the individuals running and/or owning the corporation. Judges sometimes allow plaintiffs to "pierce the corporate veil" and to win a judgment against the individuals. Crooked employees, who have helped their boss cheat the plaintiff, might be willing to "talk" in exchange for being given a promise that the lawsuit against them will be dismissed.

It is quite possible that a defendant may simply quit the business and disappear when he is sued or threatened with suit. If so, the plaintiff has probably lost nothing; the reason he sued was because he was not paid; and the industry is cleaner for having one less cheater.

Three of the information items that should be on each contract are the federal employer number of each party, the social security number of each individual signer, and the driver's license of each individual signer. These are useful items to have when trying to discover property of defendants.

SUMMARY

The means to obtain information and to use less expensive collection methods are used in the field of music publishing; they can be used in the field of movie distribution.

CHAPTER 3

COLLECTIONS

A stockholder of a major motion picture distributor compared the balance sheets of the previous two years. He said to himself, "Business must be improving. Accounts receivables in the second year are 50% higher than during the first year."

The stockholder may or may not have been correct. Quite possibly, sales may have been the same each year, but collections may have been much smaller.

Motion picture distributors must compete with each other to secure playtime in theatres. Competitive factors include, but are not limited to:
1. contractual terms
2. exhibitor's breaches of the contract which are waived by the distributor.

The contractual terms may:
1. on their face, require prompt payment.
2. on their face, allow slow payment.

For example, the contractual terms may require prompt payment the moment the exhibitor has all the information to calculate (a) box office receipts, (b) advertising expenses. Would you believe that sometimes it takes an exhibitor three months to calculate advertising expenses??? Where it does take the exhibitor a long time to calculate advertising expenses, the exhibitor bases his long delayed non-payment of net film rental on the provision in the contract which provides that payment must follow the final calculations of advertising expenses.

Sometimes a contract between a theatre chain and a distributor covers play dates in many theatres and allows for cross-collateralization of (1) box office receipts and (2) advertising expenses for all the play dates. Theoretically, a film which

makes a lot of money for all concerned during the first playdates, could be a box office disaster despite high advertising
expenses for the last playdates. The theatre chain may hold on
to net film rental due to the distributor on the first playdates,
on the theory that net film rental on these first playdates may
be offset by negative figures caused by excess advertising
expenses on the later film dates.

This might cause a distributor who has made an arrangement with a chain for playdates, from April to June, to not be
paid for the April dates until October or November.

Chains have been known to lie to distributors. A staller at
chain headquarters may claim that a certain theatre has not yet
sent in all figures; that certain theatre's manager may have sent
in all figures to headquarters many months previously.

One of the problems of **slow collections,** is that they
might easily become **no collections.** The distributor might be
starved out of business, and once the distributor is out of
business, the distributor's chance of collecting shrinks in
possibility and amount. Or, the exhibitor might go out of
business. Once the exhibitor is out of business, the chances of
his being forced to pay in full become dimmer.

One of the reasons for slow payment may be the
exhibitor's liability to make all payments on all debts; the
exhibitor pays those expenses which he must, pay to stay in
business (labor, rent) and stalls those expenses which are not
so pressing. The mere fact that an exhibitor is known to owe
money to other distributors will not necessarily discourage all
other distributors from doing business with that exhibitor.
Distribution is a cut-throat business. If mere rotten reputation
as a slow-pay low-pay no-pay exhibitor were enough to put an
exhibitor or chain out of business, then many currently active
exhibitors and chains would be out of business.

One of the reasons slow paying exhibitors stay in business
is because of the custom of paying old debts to obtain the right
to play new films. For example, an exhibitor may have played
BULLET EATING BABIES in January, was supposed to have
paid in February, still has not paid in May. Then, the same

distributor offers the exhibitor another film entitled BABY EATING BARBARIANS. If the distributor wants to play the second film, he will pay for the first. Of course, both the exhibitor and the distributor know that the exhibitor is not going to pay for the second film until many months later when the distributor has another money-making film.

Does the distributor care that he has to wait so long for his money? Yes. But the distributor also considers that his willingness to wait so long gives him a competetive edge over another distributor who won't wait and insists upon a deposit in front.

Some pictures have such potential box office value that distributors can insist on deposits, weekly minimum guaranteed rental even though the actual box office is terrible, and a minimum number of playdates (weeks during which the theatre must exhibit the picture).

At such times distributors may take advantage of their bargaining power, and exhibitors may be hurt.

The power concerning collections thus swings back and forth between exhibitors as a group vs. distributors as a group, and swings back and forth between individual exhibitors and individual distributors.

CONFIRMATION OF
BOOKING AND INVOICE

WESTERN FILM DISTRIBUTORS, INC.
839 NORTH HIGHLAND AVENUE
HOLLYWOOD, CALIFORNIA 90038
213/469-5321

OFFICE COPY

PERCENTAGE RENTAL 1   FLAT RENTAL 2

INVOICE DATE

TERMS:

PRIOR DATES CANCELLED
FROM — TO
MONTH DAY — MONTH DAY YEAR

PAYMENTS DUE

RENTAL

TAX

PLEASE PAY THIS AMOUNT

NO. OF REELS

PLAY DATES
FROM — TO
MO. DAY — MO. DAY YR.

THE ABOVE RELEASE, SUBJECT TO THE APPROVAL AND TERMS
OF THE CONTRACT COVERING IT, AND HAS BEEN BOOKED TO
YOU FOR EXHIBITION AS INDICATED.

PAYMENT MUST
BE IN OUR OFFICE
AT LEAST SEVEN
DAYS BEFORE
SHIPPING DATE.

MAKE PAYMENT TO

WESTERN FILM DISTRIBUTORS, INC
839 NORTH HIGHLAND AVENUE
HOLLYWOOD, CALIFORNIA 90038
213/469-5321

PLEASE RETURN A COPY
OF THIS INVOICE WITH YOUR
PAYMENT OR SHOW THE
THEATRE NO., RELEASE NO.
& PLAY DATES ON YOUR CHECK.

RELEASE NUMBER   TITLE

CIRCUIT

SHIP VIA

SHIPPING DATE

RETURN DATE

THEATRE NUMBER

-13-

CHAPTER 4

DAYS, WEEKS, MONTHS, SEASONS

The following are statements by distributors.

(1)   Hunting/Fishing pictures have better box office during non-hunting weeks than during hunting seasons.

(2)   Special pictures for children can fill theatres during early afternoon hours on week-ends. It pays theatres to play children's pictures at children's matinees and regular features for regular movie audiences in the evenings.

(3)   The best movie nights are Fridays and Saturdays.

(4)   Theatres should be kept open every night of the week to enable people with the movie habit to go any night they want to.

(5)   Many adults stay out of theatres during times attended by children and young adults; these adults may go Monday — Thursday nights.

(6)   Most of the motion picture audience are between 15 and 30. Pictures should be aimed at that audience.

(7)   Great pictures will pull the older audience which has lost the movie habit. That's why box office totals are so amazingly high for pictures which pull both the habitual and the older audience.

(8)   A picture shooting for Academy Awards can be released during the year preceeding the Awards, can be re-released during the months of its publicized candidacy, can be re-released the day and week following the Awards if the picture received any Oscars.

(9)   An exploitation picture, a horror picture, a Walt Disney picture, may draw a ready made and waiting audience, most of whom will see the picture during the first week the picture is available in the neighborhood. Thus a tremendous above-average box office the first week may not be a reason to keep the picture a second week. The best times for such pictures are when school is out: Thanksgiving, Christmas, between semesters, Easter vacation, Summer vacation, 3 day week-ends.

CHAPTER 5

DETECTIVE STORY

The angel sent hoods to the producer's office. The producer was sitting in his shirtsleeves. The hoods shot the producer again and again until he died. Then they put his sports jacket on the producer, sat him on his stuffed chair. Why, after killing the producer, did the hoods put on his sports jacket and place him on his stuffed chair?

Several producers have learned the hard way that angels who back pictures with equity investments and loans don't like to lose money, and sometimes express their unhappiness violently.

Other producers have gentler backers, who also lose their investments in pictures.

Several years ago, the major Hollywood production companies reported a two year loss of a half billion dollars.

Distributors with dozens to hundreds of pictures in their catalogs have gone out of the distribution business.

Many theatres have gone out of business.

Meanwhile, other angels, producers, distributors, sub-distributors, exhibitors have earned hundreds of millions of dollars. Billions are paid by movie viewers to theatre box office cashiers.

What happens to those billions?

Why do so many motion picture producers fail to receive from distributors even the costs of production?

Clues are spread throughout the book.

How can producers and distributors improve their operations and their profits?

Clues are spread throughout the book.

One clue — producers are ignorant about distribution.

Second clue — distributors are ignorant about distribution.

Third clue — there is no correlation whatsoever between (1) those who scream about other people's dishonesty, and (2) those who are honest.

What can you do to (1) improve the situation? (2) get a piece of the action?

Seek the clues!!!

CHAPTER 6

DISTRIBUTOR CONSIDERS ACCEPTING
A PICTURE

The Distributor considers:

(a)   The picture was shot in 16mm. The cost of preparing 35mm negative, etc. will be $ _____

(b)   The lab will (not) give credit.

(c)   The distributor will have to pay the lab sooner or later. The Distributor-Exhibitor-Contract provides that Producer will reimburse Distributor out of Producer's Royalties. How likely is the possibility that there will be any Producer's Royalties?

(d)   The lab has a lien on the picture for part of the cost of developing the takes, and for other work. The lien is for $ _____

(e)   The bank loan is due on _____

(f)   The bank loan is due in _____ months.

(g)   What is the chance of the picture being successful enough to allow the bank loan to be paid off in time?

(h)   Should the distributor delay distribution, or distribute slowly, so that the producer, will be forced to sell his rights in the Producer's Royalties for enough money to pay the bank loan?

(i)   Picture title.

(j)   Producer

(k)   Director

(l)   Stars

(m)   Also starring (supporting players)

(n)   Title song

(o)   Music soundtrack.

(p)   Technical matters.

(q)   Cost of acquiring picture

(r)   Cost of prints

(s)   Cost of national trade ads and other advertising to reach theatres.

(t)   Cost of advertising to reach public.

(u)   The cost of borrowing money.

(v)   Other money outlay.

(w)   Whether he can handle the picture with his existing capacity (personnel, money, etc.).

(x)   Whether the picture is right for the Distributor.   For example, a Distributor who knows how to handle X pictures, may or may not want to handle R pictures.

(y)   Other matters.

CHAPTER 7

DISTRIBUTOR – EXHIBITOR CONTRACT

1. Identification of motion picture

2. Identification of parties

3. Pricing arrangements

4. Advertising

5. Dates for receiving and returning (or forwarding) prints

6. Run

7. Clearance

8. Warranties

9. Theatre

10. Playing dates and playing times

11. Requirement of consecutively numbered tickets

12. Auditing rights

13. Freight

14. Trailers

15. Copyright rights and restrictions

16. Possible breaches and remedies

CHAPTER 8

DISTRIBUTOR – EXHIBITOR FINANCIAL TERMS

1.   4 Wall. Distributor pays Exhibitor a fee for the use of the theatre. Distributor keeps box office receipts. Distributor pays for all advertising.

2.   Flat Fee. Exhibitor pays Distributor a flat fee and keeps all box office receipts. Exhibitor pays for all advertising.

3.   Percentage. Distributor and Exhibitor agree each shall receive a percentage of the box office and allocate advertising expenses in the same percentage.

4.   Nut. 90–10. Exhibitor receives sum agreed to be house nut (cost of operating the theatre, theoretically). After that sum has been reached, box office receipts are shared: 90% to Distributor, 10% to Exhibitor. Distributor pays 90% or 100% of advertising costs.

5.   Sometimes an Exhibitor will pay a percentage of box office receipts for one film and a flat fee for a second feature.

6.   Sometimes two features will share equally the amounts received by the distributor who is booking them together as a double feature.

7.   Sometimes percentages slide, with one percentage of box office paid to a distributor up to one plateau, a higher percentage paid up to a second monetary plateau, etc.

CHAPTER 9

DISTRIBUTORS SEEK FILMS, BUT . . .

A distributor is in the business of distributing films.

A distributor has overhead which goes on whether or not he has any income. When there is no income, there may be a few cuts in personnel, space, travel. But each cut has disadvantages: the departed personnel and their knowledge may not be available when the distributor wants to expand. Space cutting may mean cramped quarters. Reduced travel may mean reduced personal contacts and personal knowledge concerning local conditions, which could mean reduced income from sales both currently and in the future.

A distibutor's personnel may consist of just one Mouth and one all around Paper Pusher, or a distributor may have many Mouths and many Paper Pushers.

Each distributor, no matter what his size may be, needs to have films to distribute, so that he can receive net film rentals.

To acquire such films: (a) some distributors make their own films in their own studios and elsewhere, (b) other distributors wholly or partially finance producers, (c) other distributors have a policy of acquiring films which have been completed, or at least partially completed, (front money may or may not be paid to acquire such films); other distributors follow several of the above and other policies.

A producer who has completed a picture may be shocked to learn that no distributor will pay him front money to obtain the rights of distribution.

Note: One distributor said that if he has to pay front money to acquire the picture, he does so **as a co-producer buying out a percentage of the producer's rights to the producer's**

share of money eventually paid by the distributor. For example, if the distributor buys out 50% of the producer.s rights, than an accounting may show:

Distributor received in Net Film Rental	$1,000,000
— All kinds of expenses discussed elsewhere	700,000
Payable to Producer (50%) and to Co-Producer (50%)	300,000
— Payable to Co-Producer (50%) (The Distributor)	150,000
Payable to Producer (50%)	$ 150,000

Sometimes producers owe money for the time they have expended all money available to make the film; such producers want distributors to pay such debts. Frequent creditors include transportation companies, credit card companies, taxing authorities, labs. Producers who borrowed money from banks   at the commencement of principal photography may have made 18 months loans; by the time the picture is completed and a few distributors have rejected the picture, the 18 month due date may be nearing.

Many producers are under pressure to save their relatives and friends, who co-signed for bank loans or co-signed lab credit application contracts, from having to pay the debts for which they co-signed.

Thus both parties are under pressure to make a deal: the distributor needs product and the producer needs a distributor.

The pressure is seldom equal. The distributor can decline a film or not close a deal without the loss of the film bothering him much; he can be fairly certain that other producers will be offering him films in the near future.

There are many completed films in film vaults which completed films have not been accepted, even without front money by any distributor.

These completed films can be divided into two classifications — (1) those which have no debts which need be paid or assumed by the distributor; (2) those which do have debts (sometimes liens) which need be paid by the distributor before he can receive the right to distribute the film.

CHAPTER 10

DISTRIBUTOR – SUB-DISTRIBUTOR CONTRACT

1. Authorizing clause. Sub-distributor is authorized to represent Distributor.

2. Territory clause. For example: (a) Florida, (b) 13 Western States.

3. Duration. For example: (a) Two years. (b) Ten years. (c) First Wednesday in October until first Tuesday in November for multiples up to 35 prints, (d) or combination or variation thereof.

4. Calculation of Sub-Distributor Share of Net Film Rentals or Other Basis.

5. Delivery dates and places.

6. Warranties.

7. Non-theatrical operations.

8. Other provisions.

9. Identification of parties.

10. Identification of motion picture.

11. Freight / Advertising / Sales Material.

CHAPTER 11

DISTRIBUTOR/SUB-DISTRIBUTOR CONTRACT

AGREEMENT, made and entered into this _____ day of
_____ , 19_____by and between _____
having an office for the transaction of business at _____
_____, Los Angeles, California, hereinafter
referred to as '**Licensor**' and _____
having its principal place of business at _____
in the City of _____ State of _____,
hereinafter referred to as the '**Licensee**':

WITNESSETH

   1. Licensor hereby grants to the Licensee and Licensee accepts,
the exclusive license under copyright to exhibit and distribute to
exhibitors for theatrical exhibition, in 35M only, the following
motion picture:

   2. TERRITORY: The territory covered by this agreement
and the franchise herein granted shall consist of the motion
picture exchange territory of:

this being the territory usually served by the majority of Motion
Picture Exchanges in above described territory. Licensor hereby
grants Licensee the right to distribute and arrange for the
exhibition and exploitation of the motion picture herein
specified in established theatres and drive-in theatres regularly
used for the exhibition of motion pictures in the above
described territory. The high seas, inland waterways, and all
ships, railroad trains and other common carriers, army, navy,
marine corps camps are excluded from and shall be deemed to
be outside the licensed territory.

   For the purpose of this Agreement, the word '**territory**'
shall be construed to mean and referred to the territory hereinabove described. No rights of any kind or nature with respect
to the motion picture outside the said territory are granted to or
shall be exercised by Licensee, all such rights being reserved to
Licensor.

3. TERM: The term of this Agreement and the franchise granted herein (unless terminated earlier) shall be for a period of two years from the date first above written.

4. DISTRIBUTION FEE: For the motion picture licensed under this Agreement the Licensee shall remit to the Licensor from the gross collections of said picture as follows:

    a. ADVANCE: Licensee shall advance $ _____ with the signing of this Agreement as its 40% share of one print cost. Additional prints to be paid for by Distributor on same percentage (40%) basis.

    b. Licensee will pay for prints at laboratory cost plus transportation charges and agrees to order _____ prints upon signing of this Agreement and to put the picture into release and distribution immediately.

    c. DISTRIBUTION FEE: Thereafter Licensee will remit to Licensor _____ (_____ %) of the gross collections of said picture.

    d. GUARANTEE: Licensee guarantees to Licensor the sum of $ _____ by the end of six months from date of this Agreement. This guarantee shall be paid to Licensor by Licensee either from collections or by a guaranteed payment of said amount. If the picture has not earned the sum of $_____ as Licensor's share in the six months time from the date hereof, Licensor shall have the right at any time thereafter to cancel this contract with Licensee upon ten (10) days written notice to Licensee and all rights of Licensee in the picture shall automatically revert to Licensor, and Licensee agrees to hold Licensor free and clear of this Agreement and agrees to deliver to Licensor all prints and advertising accessories in his possession at the time of cancellation.

5. CONDITIONS: The license hereinunder granted is personal to Licensee. Licensee may not assign, transfer, mortgage, pledge or hypothecate, directly or indirectly or by operation of law, or in any other way part or attempt to part with the license, prints or accessories referred to in this Agreement without the Licensor's prior written consent.

    If Licensee becomes involvent or makes any assignment for the benefit of creditors or if a voluntary or involuntary petition in bankruptcy is filed by or against Licensee, or any amount hereunder payable is not promptly paid when due or there is any other violation of the terms of this Agreement, or Licensee discontinues the distribution of said picture or the franchise Agreement is cancelled without fault on the part of the Licensor, the Licensor may give written notice to Licensee of the default so created and if Licensee does not cure said default within (10) ten days from the date of the mailing of such notice, this Agreement and all rights granted to Licensee hereunder shall terminate at the option of Licensor.

6. REPORTS: Licensee shall exert its best efforts and ability to the end that as many and as profitable bookings shall be had of the picture without discrimination and in the exercise of the highest good faith, and will not make the sale of any picture licensed hereunder conditioned on the sale of any other picture not owned by the Licensor. Licensee will hold Licensor's share of the gross collections at all times as Trustee for L icensor until the same shall have been paid to Licensor as provided hereunder and all reports and remittances to Licensor hereunder shall be made and payable to Licensor at his address. Licensee will furnish a statement to Licensor not later than Friday of each week, including, without limitation, reports of all receipts, contracts made, and business written each week.

7. PAYMENTS: Commencing on the first Friday next following the delivery to Licensee of the prints of the above-titled picture, and on Friday of each week thereafter, Licensee shall pay to Licensor during the term and period of license hereof, the percentage of the total gross collections as set forth in Paragraph Four (4) above, from its distribution of the picture during the preceding week. Time and prompt payments is an essence of this Agreement. Gross Collections are defined as the entire amount paid by the theatre to which the picture is rented on percentage.

8. RECORDS: Licensee shall keep and maintain, at its principal place of business, until the expiration or earlier termination of Licensee's rights or license hereunder, and for a period of three (3) years thereafter, complete detailed, permanent, true and accurate books of account and records relating to the distributing and exhibition and exploitation of the motion picture, including but without being limited to, detailed box-office receipts, detailed bookings thereof, rentals received and/or due and to grow due therefrom, gross collections derived therefrom detailed billings thereon and detailed playdates thereof, whereabouts of prints, trailers, accessories and other material in connection with the motion picture. Licensee further agrees that all such books of account shall be approved by Licensor, and Licensee further agrees to give to Licensor or its accredited representative, until the expiration or earlier termination of Licensee's rights and license hereunder, and for a period of three (3) years thereafter, access at any time to the bookings, rentals and receipts derived from the exhibition, distribution and exploitation of the motion picture, and to permit Licensor or its representatives during such time to make extracts therefrom.

9. RESERVATION OF RIGHTS: The Licensee acknowledges that there is not granted to it under this Agreement any right in television, radio, 16M or any substandard size of film. All reproduction, remake, dramatic, pictorial, scenario, dialogue, literary and music rights without any limitation whatever are reserved to the Licensor. No rights in non-theatrical exhibition are granted under this Agreement.

10. GENERAL CONDITIONS: Delivery hereunder shall mean delivery to a common carrier.

The legal ownership of the prints delivered to Licensee in accordance with Paragraph Four above shall remain with Licensor at all times and at the expiration of the term of this Agreement, Licensee shall return these prints to Licensor at Licensor's address, prepaid.

Licensee further agrees that it shall solicit and accept bookings on the picture on a percentage arrangement only in which the picture receives from the theatre a specified percentage of the gross receipts of the booking engagement and Licensee further agrees to submit all contracts on all bookings for Licensor's approval and at no time will such a contract be a binding contract with the exhibitor unless it has the signature of approval by an officer or a properly designated official of Licensor and Licensee agrees that there shall be no second feature (companion picture) allowance or deduction made on any booking unless the cost thereof is first approved by Licensor.

Nothing contained in this Agreement shall be construed as constituting a joint venture or partnership between the parties hereto and neither party shall have the authority to bind the other as its representative in any manner whatsoever unless otherwise expressly provided in this Agreement.

If any provisions of this Agreement should be declared unenforceable it shall be deemed deleted and shall not affect the enforceability of the remainder of this Agreement.

Licensee agrees to pay for all print inspection and shipping charges from its Forty (40%) percent share of collections received from playdates and hold Licensor free of any and all such charges. Licensee further agrees that the amount of film rental collected by it from theatre on each playdate is the amount on which Licensor shall receive its Sixty (60%) percent and that there shall be no deductions of any kind or nature made from the amount collected from each playdate and shall furnish Licensor with original reports and statements of such playdates as received from theatre.

IN WITNESS WHEREOF the parties to this Agreement have set their hands the day and year first above written.

By   _____

"Licensor"

By   _____

"Licensee"

WITNESS:

_____

CHAPTER 12

DISTRIBUTING PRINTS
ACTIVITIES AND EXPENSES

Distributors distribute many prints of many pictures.

Distributors have problems of inventory. Each print costs money to manufacture, to ship, to keep track of, to inspect, to warehouse. Prints may be physically handled by personnel employed by the distributor or by specialized services which perform transportation, inspection and warehousing functions for distributors.

Distributors' expenses include transportation charges to and from theatres, inventory taxes, insurance on prints and shipments, administrative costs, storage costs, handling costs, clerical costs, administrative and overhead costs.

Communication costs are high. Face to face communications may require the distributor flying around the country to see sub-distributors and exhibitors to plan and execute contracts and campaigns.

Long distance telephone rates are high, but are much lower than first class plane and hotel rates.

Teletype and telegrams are used to confirm conversations and oral arrangements.

First class mail, airmail, special delivery, priority mail, sending prints by air are all U.S. Postal Service services.

The distributor (or his shipping department) must know about firms which specialize in shipping prints, firms which ship to another airport (but don't supply airport to theatre service), bus lines which ship to bus stations (but don't supply bus station to theatre service), etc.

The whole area of distributing physical prints is involved. Persons who want to learn about the distribution of good business generally (and will then apply general principles to the film print distribution business) may enjoy:

1. UNDERSTANDING TODAY'S DISTRIBUTION CENTER by Ackerman, Gardner, Thomas. The Traffic Service Corporation. Washington, D.C. 20005.

2. ELEMENTS OF CONTRACT CARRIAGE by Bergen and Barrett. Traffic Service Corporation, Washington, D.C.20005.

3. INDUSTRIAL TRAFFIC MANAGEMENT by Wagner, Colton and Ward. Traffic Service Corporation, Washington, D.C. 20005.

The importance of transportation and communication expenses in film distribution may be illustrated by the fighting between knowledgeable producers and distributors concerning the allocation of those expenses in the producer-distributor contract. Alternatives include: 1. The expenses come out of the producer's share. 2. The expenses are absorbed by the distributor. 3. The expenses are deducted off the top **before** the computation of the base on which the distributor's share is computed.

If transportation comes out of the producer's share, it may be lucrative for the distributor to distribute the film to many marginal theatres which would not be licensed to play the film if transportation has to be paid by the distributor.

CHAPTER 13

DISTRIBUTOR "UNFAIR" AND/OR ILLEGAL PRACTICES

The most important information sought by exhibitors who are thinking of booking a film is — how well has the film done at the box office.

Exhibitors learn which theatres around the country are similar to theirs in box office receipts. If the Broadway in one city and the Bijou in another have similar box office grosses, then the Bijou will want to know how well the picture did at the Broadway.

Distributors can run correlations through their computers. Exchange personnel who know the theatres in their territory, also know which theatres are interested in box office receipts of what other theatres.

The correlation between test theatre and interested theatre need not be 1 to 1. The interested theatre may know that generally in horror pictures its gross is twice that of the test theatre, in Westerns it is the same, in Science Fiction the ratio of test to interested theatre is 1:2.5, while for million dollar hits the ratio is 1:3.

Exhibitors and exchange personnel are aware that there are innumerable other factors which influence the exhibitor in determining the highest amount in fees and percentages he is willing to pay for the right to exhibit a picture.

Some exhibitors want to see pictures before deciding on bids.

The project of screening pictures for exhibitors has advantages and disadvantages.

An advantage which the screening of an excellent picture

(excellent means that the exhibitors believe the picture will do well at the box office) can provide for the distributor is the enthusiastic auction-like atmosphere. Each exhibitor wants the picture. Each is afraid he may lose the picture.

Disadvantages to distributors of screening pictures include the expenses and include the possibility that the exhibitors will agree amongst themselves to conspire to rent the picture for a low amount.

Expenses include the communications necessary to arrange a screening, the publicizing of the screening and inviting exhibitors, costs of freight for the print, rental of the screening room, food and drink, etc.

Unfortunately, the audience for the picture is not composed of those who enjoy pictures, but of professional exhibitors who have probably seen 1000 better pictures.

Let's face it. By this time so many movies have been made that it is the rare current movie which is good enough to enter into the Top 1000. Possibly less than 10% of each year's new crop of films belong in the Top 1000.

Often, distributors really don't want to show their films to exhibitors. Often, exhibitors could not care less about screening films before they buy the right to show the films in their respective theatres. Often, exhibitors don't mind bidding blindly for films they have not seen.

After all, attending a screening is expensive for an exhibitor. He must leave his office, drive to the screening, kill time watching a variation of ten movies, and then must make decisions: (1) how well did he like the film, (2) how well will potential audiences a quarter of a century younger like the film. Telling a distributor what an exhibitor really thinks about a film can be a very unpleasant experience for both.

The trouble between distributors and exhibitors starts when distributors don't give exhibitors the opportunity to see the film before requiring bids. Exhibitors resent being forced to promise to pay cash for a film before they can see it.

This is especially troublesome when the exhibitor does not yet have his preferred source of information: box office results from test theatres.

Two practices which bothers exhibitors is block booking and tie-in bookings. A distributor who has a hot double feature and a turkey may insist that the exhibitor book the turkey for one week as a condition of the exhibitor booking the hot double feature during another week.

Bigger distributors with more hot product have bigger clouts than smaller distributors, and can force exhibitors to book more turkeys.

Block booking is now illegal. The biggest distributors did it in 1948 and before.

Tie-in booking is frowned upon by just about everybody except the producer and distributor of the weak picture which needs the tie-in in order to be played.

Theoretically, distributors are supposed to offer the opportunity to bid for the right to rent a film to all theatres.

As a practical matter, a sub-distributor or exchange may have a stereotyped map of theatres — which are first-run, multiple-run, later-run.

Sometimes this stereotype interferes with the right of each theatre to bid. For example, a theatre which never shows British pictures may not even be notified by a distributor that a British picture is available. Such failure may enable the forgotten theatre to scream "discrimination," "anti-trust violation," etc.

Powerful chains do have competetive power to persuade distributors to give them preferences in financial terms, runs, clearances, etc. Small theatres complain about such preferences. Distributors must be careful to not give little theatres proof of preferences.

Bidding may be blind. Exhibitors don't like blind bidding. Live auctions may be held, with all exhibitors being in one room.

Bids from exhibitors may be sent in writing to the distributor. The distributor may or may not give information about the terms bid to other bidders.

Whatever the practice may be, the practice has advantages and disadvantages.

If the practice favors the distributors, then the exhibitors should "Unfair. Illegal or should be illegal. Notify the Justice Department!"

Distributors know the terrible effect on the biggest producers-distributors of the 1948 Paramount case, which occurred after the Justice Department was finally persuaded to act.

Big distributors want to avoid stirring up the Justice Department.

CHAPTER 14

DRIVE-IN THEATRES

There are about five thousand drive-in theatres in the United States. The average car capacity in drive-ins is 500 — 600 cars. Drive-in theatres account for about a quarter of U.S. box office gross.

A list of drive-in theatres, by state, locality, capacity, is contained in the annual issues of the INTERNATIONAL MOTION PICTURE ALMANAC.

Some distributors use cards, sheets, files, computer data, to list:

NAME OF THEATRE
LOCALITY
STATE
OWNER

Picture / Playdate / Reported / Amount Due / Date & Amount
Gross   Received
1.
2.
. . .

The card may contain more information, depending upon its purpose. The above card supplies some information which may help the distributor calculate terms and advertising budgets for future pictures.

The same information may be useful in considering campaigns for territories.

CHAPTER 15

DISTRIBUTOR: _____

Address: _____

_____

_____

EXHIBITION CONTRACT

SCHEDULE

TITLE OF MOTION PICTURE	Consecutive Days Run		License Fee or Minimum Guarantee Against ½ of Gross Receipts per Motion Picture	
	Begin.	End.	Rental or Minimum Guarantee	½ of All Gross Receipts

TERMS:

Additional Comments:

The following together with all of the terms and conditions on the reverse side is the contract of license for the picture for which the application of the Exhibitor is accepted by the Distributor at its home office in _____.

LICENSE: The DISTRIBUTOR grants and the **EXHIBITOR** accepts a limited license under copyright to exhibit the same publicly at only the theatre on the number of consecutive days of exhibition and on only the date or dates specified in the Schedule hereof or otherwise set in accordance with the terms hereof and confirmed in writing by Distributor. Exhibitor agrees that the Picture will be exhibited and projected on each consecutive day during the entire period of its engagement and on each show of every day of the engagement from the actual opening hour of the Theatre to its closing, unless otherwise authorized by Distributor in the Schedule hereof or in writing. Unless otherwise expressly permitted in the Schedule, said license includes no right to exhibit at any time or place other than on the date or dates and at the designated theatre as above provided and confirmed in writing by Distributor. Exhibitor agrees not to sell or permit any sale or distribution of souvenir program, pictures, books, sheet music, phonograph records or any other merchandise pertaining to or in connection with the Picture, or the stars therein, at, before or during any performance of the Picture, in the Theatre or its lobby or foyer or in the vicinity of the Theatre without the written consent of Distributor.

DEFINITIONS:

ADMISSION PRICE: "Admission Price" means the respective admission price posted at the box office, for admission of an adult to a particular class or accommodation of the performance of the Picture involved.

GROSS RECEIPTS: "Gross Receipts" means ALL monies collected from the patron as required by law, received by Exhibitor at the box office or other place where admissions are sold. Gross receipts shall also include all monies collected from patrons at the box office for the availability or privilege of heating, air conditioning, playground, parking, and any other facilities, services or conveniences, as well as for, or for the availability of, or privilege of obtaining refreshments or commodities free or at a reduced rate.

DELIVERY OF PRINT(S): Distributor shall deliver one Print of each Picture to Exhibitor. For all purposes hereunder, such delivery of the Print(s) may be effected by delivery thereof either to Exhibitor ot its authorized agent at Distributor's office servicing Exhibitor or to a common carrier, or to the United States Postal Authorities. Exhibitor shall immediately upon termination of the License Period return the print(s) together with the reels and container to Distributor at its office in the same condition as when received, reasonable wear and tear resulting from proper use thereof upon proper equipment excepted, and pay transportation charges both ways, except if Exhibitor be directed to forward the Print(s) elsewhere, it shall forward the Print(s) as directed, transportation charges collect. If Exhibitor fails to promptly so return or forward the Print(s), it shall promptly upon demand, pay any and all damages caused thereby.

DEFINITIONS — PAYMENTS — TICKETS — BOX OFFICE STATEMENTS — BOOKS and RECORDS — CHECKING:

1. Under this agreement (a) the term "engagement" shall mean the aggregate number of days specified in the schedule or selected as herein provided for which the Picture is licensed and booked for exhibition at a designated theatre, (b) the term "flat rental picture" shall mean a picture for which the film rental is a fixed sum, (c) the term "percentage picture" shall mean a picture for which the film rental is to be determined in whole or in part upon a percentage of the gross receipts or upon a guaranty and a percentage of the gross receipts, or on a fixed royalty per person admitted on each exhibition date of such engagement of the picture, (d) the term "gross receipts" shall mean all moneys received by Exhibitor, directly or indirectly, irrespective of the time or place of such receipt, for the privilege of gaining admission to the theatre on each day of the engagement of the percentage picture from the opening to the closing of the theatre on such day, and unless otherwise provided in the Schedule hereof or consented to in writing by Distributor.

2. Exhibitor agrees to pay the film rental for each picture licensed hereunder at Distributor's address as follows: (a) the fixed sum if a flat rental picture or the guaranty, if any, if a percentage picture, at least three (3) days in advance of the date of delivery of a print to Exhibitor, at Distributor's address (b) the Distributor's share on a percentage picture, immediately upon the close of the engagement or, if requested by Distributor, immediately after the close of each exhibition date of the engagement or weekly or as otherwise provided.

3. During the entire engagement of each percentage picture, Exhibitor agrees: to use only serially numbered tickets consecutively numbered in arabic numerals with the serial number printed on each half of the face of the ticket, each of which tickets shall also bear all admission taxes, if any, the net price exclusive of admission taxes, the total of such price and taxes, and the name and location of said theatre, with a separate and distinct series for each admission price classification whether or not taxable; to use no more than one series for each admission price classification at

any time without duplicates; to issue to each person admitted a separate such ticket consecutively in the numerical order of the particular series and not to reuse such tickets, and to tear each ticket on its presentation and return one stub containing the entire serial number to the patron.

4. As to each percentage picture, Exhibitor shall deliver at Distributor's address immediately after the last showing of each day of the engagement or as otherwise agreed on itemized "box office statement" signed by or on behalf of the Exhibitor (and if requested by Distributor, upon forms furnished by Distributor) which shall report in full all information requested by Distributor. Said box office statement shall certify, among other items, separately to each exhibition date and for each admission price classification on each date, the total attendance in each classification, the total attendance admitted through or on passes, only upon prior written agreement, the net price per admission, exclusive of any admission taxes, in each classification, and the gross receipts therefrom, all such admission taxes per admission as may be payable by the patron in each classification, and the receipts therefrom, the opening and closing serial number of each sequence of tickets sold or issued, other motion pictures exhibited and other entertainment of whatever kind presented at the theatre, only upon prior written agreement, the opening and closing time of the theatre, and the commencement time of each exhibition of the percentage Picture during each exhibition date.

5. The Exhibitor agrees to keep and preserve for at least four years accurate books and records showing the acquisition, disposition and supply of all tickets used or intended for admission, and separately for each admission date and for each admission price classification on each admission date, the various items required to be shown on the Exhibitor's "box office statement" to Distributor as described in the preceding paragraph, as well as any other item bearing or which bears upon the film rental due and payable or paid to Distributor on a percentage picture. Distributor shall have the right during or at any time or times subsequent to an engagement of a percentage picture to audit all of Exhibitor's books and records which may bear upon or pertain to the income of the theatre operation and may pertain to or be useful in determining the correct and accurate gross receipts or admission upon which Distributor's film rental is determined, as well as all entries concerning

operating expenses if operating expenses are an element in computing the film rental, from which operating expenses such income as renting and subrenting space in the building shall be deducted. In addition, Distributor through its own representatives or others shall have the right to check attendance, ticket issuance and gross receipts derived on each exhibition date of the engagement licensed hereunder, and for these purposes shall have full access to the theatre including the box office and all methods and apparatus for dispensing and collecting tickets for admission.

6. The exercise by Distributor of any of the right herein granted or the acceptance by Distributor of any payment or statement by Exhibitor shall be without prejudice to any of Distributor's rights and remedies and shall not prevent Distributor from thereafter disputing the accuracy of any such payment or statement made by Exhibitor, or examing the records of exhibitor as set forth herein.

7. All information obtained under this clause shall be treated as confidential by Distributor except in any arbitration or litigation.

TAXES: Exhibitor agrees to pay Distributor, where such payment is required by law to be made by Distributor, or to the taxing authority (in any instance where such tax is required to be paid directly by Exhibitor to such authority) the amount of all taxes imposed by any statute or ordinance, now in effect or hereafter enacted, levied or based upon the license, delivery, exhibition, possession or use by Exhibitor of any print of said picture, or upon the grant or exercise of this license, or based upon or measured by the license fees or any part thereof however determined, paid or payable by Exhibitor under this agreement. "TAXES" as used in this article shall be deemed to include but shall not be limited to taxes, fees, assesments, charges, levies, excises, however designated whether as a sales, gross income, gross receipts, storage, use, consumption, license, compensating excise or privilege tax or other like designations. If the exact amount of any tax is not definitely fixed or cannot be exactly determined, Distributor may estimate the amount of such tax and Exhibitor shall pay Distributor such estimated amount upon demand therefor, provided that upon final determination of the exact amount Exhibitor shall be entitled to repayment or credit for any amount paid in excess of the tax.

PLAYDATES: If playdates are not specifically set forth herein, the picture(s) licensed hereunder shall be exhibited within a reasonable period (which period shall not exceed thirty (30) days) after the picture(s) are made advailable. If Exhibitor fails to exhibit the picture(s) licensed hereunder within such reasonable period, he will be deemed to have breached this agreement and Distributor shall have the right to cancel said agreement as to any or all such picture(s) and to recover damages for all losses sustained as a result of such breach.

CLEARANCE AND RUN: (a) Subject to the provisions of paragraph (b) and (d) of this article, Distributor agrees not to exhibit or grant a license to exhibit said motion picture for exhibition in conflict with the run or clearance, if any, specified in the Schedule. Clearance as to each of said motion pictures shall be computed from the last date of exhibition thereof licensed hereunder; (b) Distributor shall the right to exhibit or grant a license to exhibit any of said motion pictures, at any time prior to the exhibition thereof hereunder, as a "preview," or a special "midnight" exhibition, or as a "pre-release," "special engagement," "merchandising engagement" or any other type of engagement prior to the general release thereof. Any such exhibition shall not be deemed a run of said motion picture, nor shall the run, availability or clearance provided herein with respect to said motion picture be governed thereby or computed therefrom.

(c) If Exhibitor is granted a second or subsequent run, the same shall not be exclusive unless so expressly specified in the Schedule and Distributor may license as many of the same runs and as many prior and subsequent runs as it may desire. If Distributor so requires, Exhibitor shall exhibit any motion picture licensed hereunder for an earlier run than herein provided. (d) Nothing herein to the contrary shall prevent Distributor from licensing any other exhibitor to or from exhibiting said picture(s) at the same time outside of a ten (10) mile radius of the theatre named herein.

TIME OF EXHIBITION: This license does not include (a) any right to exhibit prior to 6:00 A.M. on the first exhibition date of each respective motion picture, nor (b) any right of exhibition other than on the respective date or dates of exhibition determined as provided hereunder and confirmed in writing by Distributor.

DISTRIBUTOR'S RENTAL TO BE HELD IN TRUST: The

amount due Distributor on a percentage picture, or on a flat rental picture not paid for in advance for which credit has been extended by Distributor, shall belong to and be the property of the Distributor out of the first gross receipts from patrons during the engagement of any picture, the same to be held in trust by Exhibitor for Distributor, and such ownership by Distributor shall not be questioned whether or not the Exhibitor has physically segregated the moneys so collected. Should the gross receipts so collected and turned over to Distributor not be equal to the amount of license fees payable hereunder to Distributor, the Exhibitor shall nevertheless continue to be liable to Distributor for the balance of the film rental due. Nothing contained herein shall constitute Distributor and Exhibitor as general, limited or special partners, or joint ventures, for any purpose, nor shall Distributor be liable in any manner whatever to any third person for any act or omission on the part of the Exhibitor, the Exhibitor's agents or employees, or any other person in connection with the operation of said theatre.

IN WITNESS WHEREOF THE EXHIBITOR, below named, by his duly authorized representative has executed this application on the date below indicated.

Date executed   Theatre   City & State
Exhibitor   _____
        An Individual — A Partnership — A Corporation
                (STRIKE OUT TWO)
Accepted, Approved and Countersigned   Date _____

Distributor by _____
        Vice President or Sales Manager

TICKETS OF ADMISSIONS: As to each percentage picture, Exhibitor agrees: (a) to use only serially numbered tickets issued at the theatre box office, for regular, reduced rate and pass admissions, whether or not the admissions be taxable, with a separate and distinct series in a separate color for each such admission classification (b) to imprint on each half of the ticket its serial number, the name of only one theatre and town of its location to which admission thereby is available, the established box office price exclusive of admission taxes, each admission tax payable thereon, the total of such price and taxes, and if admission be free or at a lesser rate than of the established box office price, the amount exclusive of taxes actually paid, whether as a service charge, reduced rate of admission, or otherwise, the taxes actually paid thereon, if any and the total of such admission and taxes actually paid; (c) that a separate such ticket be issued at the theatre box office to each person admitted, consecutively in the order of the serial number of the particular series, of which numbers there shall be no duplicates, that no person shall be admitted except upon presentation of the ticket above provided, which ticket shall be torn in half upon presentation for admission in such manner as to return to patron a full stub bearing the entire serial number and other information above provided, with the remaining half ticket to be kept by theatre.

RECORDS: The Exhibitor agrees to keep and preserve for at least four (4) years, for possible inspection and audit at any time or times by Distributor, complete and accurate books, records and accounts including financial, tax and banking statements and records, bearing upon the daily income from the operation of the theatre, which shall enable the Distributor by appropriate audit to verify the accuracy of the box office statements submitted by the Exhibitor to the Distributor, and which shall show, among other items, for each regular, pass and reduced rate admission classification on each exhibition date, the daily attendance, sales of admissions, ticket issuance and collection, gross receipts, and license fee paid, including the various other items required in the preceding paragraph to be included in Exhibitor's daily box office statement to Distributor, also, all records, correspondence and information pertaining to the acquisition, supply and deposition of all tickets used or intended for admission to the theatre.

Distributor is hereby given the right to audit all of

Exhibitor's books and records at any time after the conclusion of the engagement of any percentage picture, and for such purpose Distributor by its authorized representative shall be given access to the theatre, including the box office, and/or other places where such books and records shall show, among other items, the number of admissions and gross receipts of each separate performance during the engagement of any percentage picture, matinee, evening and any other performances, and it is further agreed that if Exhibitor's operating expense is an element in the computation of the amount payable to Distributor hereunder the right granted herein to Distributor to audit Exhibitor's books and records shall include the right to examine all of such books and records relating to Exhibitor's operating expenses. If complete and accurate records as above provided, are made available to Distributor or its authorized representative for any audit provided for herein, copies of federal, state, or local income returns need not be submitted for such audit. The option shall be with the Distributor, in any event, if requested, all of said documents shall be made available for inspection in any litigation involving the license fee payable on a percentage picture.

CUTTING OR ALTERATION OF PRINTS: (a) The Exhibitor shall exhibit each picture in its entirety and shall not copy, duplicate, subrent or part with possession of any print thereof nor shall the Exhibitor cut or alter the same, excepting to make necessary repairs thereto, and the Exhibitor shall return each print in the same condition as received, reasonable wear only excepted; (b) The Exhibitor agrees that it will exhibit the print and motion picture exactly as delivered to it and that it will make no modifications, interpolations, adaptations, alterations, additions, eliminations or changes of any kind in the said print or motion picture, including titles, sub-titles and copyright notices. The print and motion picture will be exhibited only in the same order, arrangement, sequence and manner as appears in the print including titles, sub-titles and copyright notices.

ADVERTISING MATERIAL: Exhibitor agrees that all advertising materials which Exhibitor may lease from Distributor will be used only in conjunction with the exhibition of the respective pictures identified in such materials at the theatre or theatres specified in the Schedule, and only for the purpose of properly advertising and exploiting said respective pictures at said theatre or theatres. Exhibitor agrees not to trade, sublease, sell, give away, nor otherwise use or permit others to use such advertising material.

LOSS AND DAMAGE TO PRINTS: The Exhibitor shall pay to the Distributor a sum equal to the cost of replacement of each linear foot of any print, lost, stolen, destroyed or injured in any way in the interval between the delivery to the Exhibitor and the receipt by Distributor thereof. Such payment, however, shall not transfer title to or any interest in any such print to the Exhibitor or any other party, nor release the Exhibitor from any liability arising out of any breach of this agreement. The Exhibitor shall immediately notify the Distributor's address by telegram of the loss, theft or destruction of, or damage or injury to any print. If any print shall be received from the Exhibitor by the Distributor or any subsequent Exhibitor in a damaged or partially destroyed condition it shall be deemed to have been so damaged or destroyed by the Exhibitor unless the latter, immediately after the first public exhibition thereof, shall have telegraphed the Distributor's address that such print was received by the Exhibitor in a damaged or partially destroyed condition, setting forth fully the nature of such damage and the amount of footage so damaged or destroyed.

DAMAGES FOR BREACH: If Exhibitor violates any of the provisions of this agreement or becomes insolvent or is adjudicated bankrupt or executes an assignment for creditors or a receiver is appointed for any of Exhibitor's property, or if Exhibitor violates or fails to perform any of the provisions of any other exhibition contract(s) heretofore or hereafter made with Distributor, or any of its affiliates or subsidiaries (hereinafter referred to as causes for termination) then, in any of said events Distributor may if Exhibitor does not cure, correct or remedy the said causes for termination within seven (7) days after the happening of any such event (1) terminate the contract, (2) terminate this and such other contracts with Exhibitor. Said remedies shall be in addition to and without prejudice to any right or remedy Distributor has at law, in equity, or provided for elsewhere in this agreement on account of any such violation or breach. If Exhibitor fails or refuses to pay any license fee due under this or any other contract, Distributor may declare such failure or refusal a breach of this entire contract or a breach of this and such other contract(s) with the Exhibitor. In the event, however, a print of another picture is scheduled for delivery for exhibition pursuant to this or any other contract within fourteen (14) days after the event causing the right of termination as herein set forth, then the period during which the Exhibitor must cure, correct or remedy the said cause for termination shall be three (3) days prior to the date for delivery of the said picture.

If payment hereunder of the license fee of any Picture shall be computed either in whole or in part upon a percentage of the gross receipts of said theatre and if Exhibitor fails or refuses to exhibit any Picture for the full period as herein provided, the Exhibitor shall pay to Distributor for each day (less than one (1) week) that the Picture is not played, on the basis of the following assumed gross receipts, the percentage of gross receipts payable as film rental as set forth on the Schedule hereof: (a) If said last day is a week day, not a holiday, 300% of the last days' gross receipts for Saturday, 200% for Sunday and legal holidays and 100% for other days; and (b) If said last day is a Sunday or legal holiday, 150% of the last days' gross receipts for Saturday, 100% for Sunday and legal holidays, and 50% for other days; and (c) If said last day is a Saturday 33 1/3% of the last days' gross receipts for weekdays, 66 2/3% for Sunday and legal holidays.

If Exhibitor shall exhibit the picture for less than the full number of weeks provided for in this license, Exhibitor shall pay for each such week that the picture is not exhibited, the percentage of gross receipts payable as film rental calculated upon an assumed gross receipts equal to the last week of the engagements' gross receipts or reduced by 20% of such gross receipts per week for each week that Exhibitor fails to exhibit the picture. If the license provides for a guarantee against a percentage the film rental due in accordance with the above shall in no event be less than the guarantee. A sworn statement of said daily gross receipts shall be delivered by the Exhibitor to the Distributor upon demand therefor, signed by the Exhibitor or his manager and countersigned by cashier or treasurer. If the Distributor violates any provision hereof with respect to any Picture licensed hereunder then the Distributor shall be liable to the Exhibitor for the Exhibitor's damage which, however, shall not be in excess of the profits that would have been earned by the Exhibitor from the exhibition of the particular picture had the Distributor fully complied its obligations with respect to each picture less the profit of its Exhibitor from any substitute attraction. Any claim by the Exhibitor with respect to the condition of a print shall be deemed waived by the Exhibitor unless telegraphic notice of said claim shall have been given to the Distributor's address immediately prior to the first public exhibition thereof by the Exhibitor.

PREVENTION OF PERFORMANCE: If Exhibitor shall be prevented from exhibiting any of said motion pictures hereunder by strikes or other labor disputes, fires, or by any cause beyond Exhibitor's control, such failure of performance shall be excused, until such time as said motion picture shall be available for exhibition or by mutual agreement.

If Distributor shall be delayed or prevented from performing this agreement by strikes or other labor disputes, fires, censor rulings, unavailability of prints or by any cause beyond Distributor's control, such delay or prevention shall be excused and Distributor shall not be liable therefor.

DELIVERY C.O.D.: Exhibitor hereby authorizes Distributor to deliver the print of any Picture licensed hereunder on C.O.D. for an amount equal to the film rental, if any, then due Distributor for each picture plus, at Distributor's option, any film rental due Distributor on any other picture or pictures licensed under this and any other agreement or agreements between Distributor and Exhibitor.

ASSIGNMENT: Exhibitor may not assign without written consent of Distributor and the asignee's written acceptance. Distributor's consent to assignment by Exhibitor shall not relieve Exhibitor of liability hereunder unless Distributor specifically releases Exhibitor therefrom in writing. The sale or disposal or continuance of operation by Exhibitor of the theatre designated in this schedule prior to exhibition of the picture(s) licensed hereunder shall not relieve Exhibitor of its obligations hereunder.

WAIVER: The waiver by either party of any breach or default by the other shall not be construed as a waiver of any other or subsequent breach or default by such other party.

ACCEPTANCE OF APPLICATION: This instrument is only an application for license, and not binding until accepted in writing without alteration by offering hereto the written or a facsimile signature of an officer of or other person duly authorized by Distributor to sign this agreement. Acceptance or deposit of any check or other consideration given by Exhibitor or delivery of a print or sending of a notice of availability, or furnishing of accessories, shall not be deemed acceptance hereof.

Unless notice of acceptance is sent to Exhibitor by mail or telegram within thirty (30) days after date hereof, this application shall be deemed withdrawn. Upon acceptance as above provided, a duplicate copy signed by Distributor shall be forwarded to Exhibitor. Approval or rejection of this application shall not be deemed an approval or rejection of any other application signed by Exhibitor at the same time or at any other time.

VERBAL PROMISES, CHANGES MUST BE IN WRITING: This license agreement is complete, and all promises, representations, understandings and agreements in reference thereto have been expressed herein. THE PROVISIONS HEREIN, INCLUDING, BUT NOT LIMITED TO THE FILM RENTAL PROVISIONS, SHALL NOT BE AFFECTED BY ANY COURSE OF DEALING OR USAGE OF THE TRADE, ACTUAL OR ALLEGED, NOR SHALL ANY COURSE OF DEALING OR USAGE OF THE TRADE, ACTUAL OR ALLEGED, BE CONSIDERED IN DETERMINING THE MEANING OF OR TO EXPLAIN OR SUPPLEMENT OR QUALIFY ANY UNAMBIGUOUS PROVISIONS OF THIS WRITING. There are no representations or warranties, express or implied, of title against infringement or of merchantability, fitness or otherwise, which extend beyond the description on the face hereof and which are not expressly set forth herein. All prior negotiations and agreements are merged herein. No change, modification or assignment hereof shall be binding against the Distributor unless in writing and signed by its general sales manager or an officer of Distributor.

Should Exhibitor fail to pay for the prints as hereinabove provided, it is understood and agreed between the parties that said prints are the sole property of Distributor and that Exhibitor shall obtain only the right to the use of said prints pursuant to the terms of this agreement. Upon the completion of the showing of said picture by Exhibitor pursuant to this agreement, Exhibitor agrees to immediately return any and all prints received by Exhibitor to Distributor.

Distributor agrees to defend or to provide for the defense arising from the showing of said film pursuant to the terms of this agreement with respect to any criminal action brought by or on behalf of any federal, state or municipal agency, against any exhibitor of said film or persons acting on behalf of said exhibitor. Distributor reserves the right to first provide an attorney to handle said defense , and, if such cannot reasonably be provided, to have the right of approval of any attorney selected of any such person desiring defense prior to Distributor's obligation under the provisions of this agreement.

Exhibitor will provide the service of distributing, and, if necessary, forwarding to Distributor any questionnaires or surveys conducted by Distributor during the term of the exhibition of this film, provided, however, that Distributor will pay all mailing costs.

Should the parties agree that Exhibitor sell any material during the showing of said film then the attached Exhibit "A" shall be executed and become a part of this agreement.

_____

_____

INITIALS

EXHIBIT "A"

The parties herein agree that Exhibitor shall sell that certain book entitled _____ during the showing of the film entitled _____, pursuant to the terms of that written agreement to which this exhibit is attached under the following provisions:

A.   All copies of said book shall be provided by Distributor or his authorized assignee or representative.

B.   Said book shall be sold for not less than $------------ per copy.

C.   Said book shall not be sold to anyone under the age of twenty-one (21) years.

D.   The proceeds from the sale of said book shall be divided _____ .

Said proceeds shall be delivered to Distributor each and every _____ , accompanied by a signed statement of account showing the number of books sold and the receipts.

E.   Upon the termination of the written agreement to which this exhibit is attached, for any reason, Exhibitor agrees to immediately deliver to Distributor any and all copies of said book in the possession of Exhibitor and to pay immediately for all books received by Exhibitor and not returned.

F.   It is understood that the ownership of said book shall at all times reside in Distributor and that Exhibitor shall receive only the right to sell the book under the terms and conditions of this exhibit and the agreement to which this exhibit is attached.

DATED:

"Distributor"

_____

"Exhibitor"

_____

INSTITUTE FOR ADULT EDUCATION
P.O. BOX 2710, HOLLYWOOD, CALIFORNIA 90028

EXHIBITOR'S REPORT OF
PERCENTAGE ENGAGEMENT

THEATRE

PICTURE NO.   CIRCUIT   PICTURE TITLE   ACCT. NO.

TERMS

PLAY DATE   WK

SECOND FEATURE

TITLE   COST

ATTENTION, PLEASE!

YOUR CONTRACT REQUIRES YOU TO FILL IN COMPLETE
ITEMIZED INFORMATION ON THIS REPORT AND

RETURN IT IMMEDIATELY

AFTER THE LAST SHOWING OF THE PICTURE, ATTACHING
CHECK FOR FILM RENTAL DUE.

THIS IS IMPORTANT!

PLEASE MAKE YOUR CHECK FOR FILM RENTAL
PAYABLE TO INSTITUTE FOR ADULT EDUCATION

DETAIL OF NUMBER OF TICKETS SOLD AND DAILY BOX OFFICE RECEIPTS (EXCLUDING ALL TAXES ON ADMISSIONS)

DAY AND DATE	TICKET DATA	NUMBER @ ¢		NUMBER @ ¢		NUMBER @ ¢		NUMBER @ ¢		NUMBER @ ¢		TOTAL DAILY RECEIPTS
		TICKET NUMBERS	TOTAL NO. SOLD	TICKET NUMBERS	TOTAL NO. SOLD	TICKET NUMBERS	TOTAL NO. SOLD	TICKET NUMBERS	TOTAL NO. SOLD	TICKET NUMBERS	TOTAL NO. SOLD	
	CLOSE NO.											$
	OPEN NO.											
	CLOSE NO.											

—52—

OPEN NO.							
CLOSE NO.							
OPEN NO.							
CLOSE NO.							
OPEN NO.							
CLOSE NO.							
OPEN NO.							
CLOSE NO.							
OPEN NO.							
TOTALS							$

—53—

MISCELLANEOUS:

BREAKDOWN OF ADMISSION PRICES

TOTAL PAID ADMISSION	FED. TAX	OTHER TAX	NET ADM.

DEDUCTIONS PER CONTRACT

FOR

FOR

NET PARTICIPATING RECEIPTS

DISTRIBUTOR'S SHARE

% OF

NET FILM RENTAL

CERTIFIED AS CORRECT BY:

THEATRE CASHIER

EXHIBITOR

DATE

FORM 2A

RETURN ORIGINAL AND ONE COPY TO INSTITUTE FOR ADULT EDUCATION.

CHAPTER 16

EXHIBITOR – CUSTOMER CONTRACT

This contract is partly written (the ticket), mostly established by custom.

    1. Parties – Customer
                    Exhibitor
    2. Price – Varies by classification of customer into
(a) Adult, (b) Student, (c) Child, (d) Senior, (e) Pass.
            – Varies by time of day, for example:
(a) Before 1 PM, (b) Before 6 PM, (c) Evening.

    3. Customer receives the right to sit in a seat during
(a) only one complete program, or (b) as long as the theatre is open.

    4. Customer receives right to see the picture.

    5. Exhibitor has written (No smoking in this area) and unwritten rules (good behavior required), and may throw out rule breaking customers.

CHAPTER 17

EXHIBITOR-DISTRIBUTOR-PRODUCER MONOPOLISTS

From the 1920s to the 1940s, several companies were leaders in all three fields: they owned many of the largest theatres, and owned or co-owned many small theatres; they produced pictures in their own studios; they distributed pictures.

In 1943-1944, five national distributors each had more than 10% of the market: Fox, Loew's, Paramount, RKO, Warner. Six distributors had just about the rest of the market: Columbia, United Artists, Universal, Republic, Monogram, PRC.

In 1945, over 100 theatres were owned by each of the following: Paramount 1395; Warner 501; Loew's 135; Fox 636; RKO 109; joint ownerships 361.

For further information, you can read: (1) ANTITRUST IN THE MOTION PICTURE INDUSTRY, Economic and Legal Analysis.
(2) UNITED STATES v. PARAMOUNT PICTURES, 70 Federal Supplement 53 (1947)
(3) UNITED STATES v. PARAMOUNT PICTURES, 334 United States Reports 131 (1948).

In 1948, the United States Supreme Court determined that there should be a divorce between production and exhibition, calling the marriage a monopoly.

Eventually, there was such a divorce.

After the divorce, there were attempts of re-marriage.

Theatres complain about a product shortage.

A theatre which plays two distinct double feature programs weekly (Sunday — Wednesday, Thursday — Saturday), plays 4 films weekly, 208 annually.

If there are two or three theatres near each other, or twin or tri-plex theatres, each will want product not played in the other theatres. 208 films times 2 theatres equals 416; 208 films times 3 theatres equal 624 films.

In pre-divorcement days, more features were released than in current days. For example, in 1945, a total of 388 films were released by the following distributors: Loew's 50, Fox 59, Paramount 58, Warner 53, RKO 49, Columbia 55, Universal 46, United Artists 18.

The exhibitors have adjusted to the shortage by changing their policies concerning the number of days or weeks a film stays in the theatre. Twice-weekly changes have given way to weekly changes. Many theatres play the same film week after week. The saving in freight for prints and in not changing the marque are minor; often an exhibitor keeps a film because he simply can't find another film which shows better promise.

Some exhibitors decide, from time to time, to decrease the picture shortage by producing pictures.

National General and American Broadcasting, two theatre-owning circuits, embarked on ambitious film-making programs in 1967; after four years they sharply curtailed their film-making programs. Why? Possibly, because wearing their hats as Producers and Distributors, they did not have much "luck."

CHAPTER 18

EXHIBITOR SPEAKS TO DISTRIBUTOR
ABOUT SUB-DISTRIBUTOR

"I saw my sub-distributor in a Southern state. If you think Dracula is a monster, you have not seen my sub-distributor."
Identification withheld.

Exhibitor to Distributor: "Your sub told you that I had not paid him? Here is my cancelled check to your Sub; see his endorsement. Here is my letter of transmittal identifying your picture as the picture I was paying for. I paid your Sub. He lied to you when he said I did not pay him.

"I pay all distributors. Sometimes I am short of cash and I can't pay everybody. Then I pay the most powerful distributors, the majors. I can't afford to let a major withhold 10–15 pictures a year from me as punishment for not paying promptly.

"Your sub-distributor handles about 20 pictures a year. In this area, your sub is as powerful as a major. I can't afford to have him withhold 20 pictures a year from me as punishment for not paying promptly.

"I need product every week. Some pictures are strong enough to stand up for a second week. But I would rather play a new picture or double feature every week.

"I need to be a better customer than any of my competitors, so that the major's exchanges and the independent sub-distributors prefer dealing with me to dealing with my competitors. One way I can be a better customer is to pay promptly.

"I know my week's box office receipts on Tuesday night. I know the cost of advertising when I order it, and that's before and possibly during the picture's run. On Wednesday morning I know my take, my expenses, the terms of the contract. I calculate the amount I have to pay, and I pay it.

"The sub-distributor is entitled to one-fourth of the net film rental. He may be entitled to some reimbursement of some small expense. There is nothing to stop him from paying the national distributor 50% of what I paid on the day the sub received my check. The rest of what the sub owes to the distributor could be calculated and paid at the end of the month.

"The villain in the whole distribution business is the sub-distributor. He is not worth 25% of net film rental, so his fee is too high. He holds on to money due to the distributor. He gives fraudulent figures to the distributor.

"I don't give fraudulent figures to the sub. He knows my theatre. He would know if my figures were false. But the sub gives fraudulent figures to the distributor. The distributor does not know my theatre. He does not know that the figures are false.

"I would be quite willing to pay half of net film rental to the sub and to pay the oher half of net film rental to the distributor. Paying two checks instead of one does not bother me. Making a simple calculation such as dividing a sum in half does not bother me. I might be bothered if I had to do more complicated math or if the percentage varied with each picture or each distributor. Or, I might not be bothered. The exhibition contract calls for a lot of math. One more calculation might not bother me.

"If the exhibition contract calls for it, I can send a copy of my box office reports to the distributor and the sub-distributor at the same time.

"The situation is serious. Cheating sub-distributors and distributors cause producers to be able to produce less and cause a product shortage. It causes me to be at the mercy of distributors."

CHAPTER 19

FOUR-WALL THEATRES

There are about ten thousand four-wall theatres regularly exhibiting motion pictures.

Many theatres close; others open.

The remodelling of old large theatres into twins or 3-part or 4-part is expensive. Prints of different pictures must be acquired by multiple theatres. One manager can usually operate a multiple as easily as a single picture palace.

If timing is right, then intervals between shows will be different for each theatre of a multiple; thus the candy counter personnel will be busy constantly.

Audiences may habitually come to multiples in the expectation that at least one theatre is shown an acceptable film.

If the film in Theatre I is a tremendous box office attraction, all seats may be filled and latecomers may prefer seating in Theatre II to waiting their turn to see the picture in Theatre I.

On the other hand, the picture in Theatre II may suffer if its logical audience comes to the box office and at the last minute decides it wants to see the picture in Theatre I.

Many four-wall twin theatres are being built in shopping centers. Some Shopping Center builders are wary of theatres as financial risks. If a theatre goes out of business, then the cost of re-constructing it as a store may be very expensive.

A shopping center which has stores open generally between 10:00 AM and 6:00 PM may want the theatre hours to be after 6:00 PM to avoid over-crowding the parking lot.

There are many different kinds of four-wall theatres, which vary in seating capacity, from about 40 (such as the Bijou in Hollywood) to about 6000 (such as Radio City Music Hall in New York).

The Branch (of the major Distributor) and the Sub-Distributor (for the independent Distributor) must know each theatre, its capacity, the box office records for various kinds of films, the application of theoretical terms to the theatre, the speed of payment, past conduct of demanding settlement of previously agreed prices, the ownership of the theatre, etc.

CHAPTER 20

FRANCHISE AGREEMENT

THIS AGREEMENT, made and entered into this_____
day of _____ 19 _____ , by and between _____
having an office for the transaction of business at _____
hereinafter referred to as "Licensor," and _____ ,
having its principal place of business at _____ ,
hereinafter referred to as "Licensee":

WITNESSETH:

1. Licensor hereby grants to Licensee, and Licensee accepts
the exclusive license under copyright to exhibit and distribute
to exhibitors for theatrical exhibition, the following motion
pictures:

_____

_____

_____

etc.

2. **TERRITORY**: The territory covered by This Agreement, and the franchise herein granted, shall consist of:

_____

_____

For the purpose of This Agreement, the word "territory"
shall be construed to mean and refer to the territory hereinabove
described. No rights of any kind or nature with respect to the
motion picture outside the said territory are granted to and
shall be exercised by Licensee, all such rights being reserved
to Licensor.

In the event of any dispute with reference to territorial
boundaries, the decision of the Licensor shall be final.

3. **TERM**: Term of This Agreement and the franchise
granted herein shall be for a period of _____ years from
the date first above written.

4. **DISTRIBUTION FEE**: For the motion picture licensed

under This Agreement, Licensee shall remit to Licensor, from the gross collections derived from the distribution of said picture, as follows:

a. **DEDUCTIONS**: Licensee will pay for _____ prints at laboratory costs, plus express charges, and censorship fees and seals, if any, and deduct said amounts from gross receipts.

b. **DISTRIBUTION FEE**: Thereafter, Licensee will remit to Licensor _____ of the gross collection of said licensed picture.

c. **SPECIAL CLAUSE**: _____

---

5. CONDITIONS: The license hereunder granted is personal to Licensee. Licensee may not assign, transfer, mortgage, pledge or hypothecate, directly or indirectly, or by operation of law, or in any other way, part or attempt to part with the license, prints, or accessories referred to in This Agreement, or attempt so to do without Licensor's prior written consent.

If Licensee becomes insolvent or makes any assignment for the benefit of creditors, or if a voluntary or involuntary petition in bankruptcy is filed by or against Licensee, or any amount hereunder payable is not promptly paid when due, or there is any other violation of the terms of This Agreement, or Licensee discontinues the distribution of said picture, or the Franchise Agreement is cancelled without fault on the part of Licensor, the Licensor may give written notice to Licensee of the default so created, and if Licensee does not cure said default within ten (10) days from the date of the mailing of such notice, This Agreement and all rights granted to Licensee hereunder shall terminate at the option of Licensor.

6. REPORTS: Licensee will exert its best efforts and ability to the end that as many and as profitable bookings as possible shall be had of the picture, without discrimination, and in the exercise of the highest good faith, and will not make the sale of any picture licensed hereunder conditioned on the sale of any other picture not owned by Licensor. Licensee will hold Licensor's share of the gross collections, at all times, as Trustee for Licensor, until the same shall have been paid to Licensor, as provided hereunder, and all reports and remittances to Licensor hereunder shall be made to and paid to Licensor at its office, until and unless Licensor shall hereafter designate. Licensee will furnish a statement to Licensor not later than Friday of each week, in accordance with Weekly Report Form furnished by Licensor.

7. **PAYMENTS**: Commencing on the first Friday next following delivery of the prints of the above entitled picture to Licensee, and the term and period of license hereof, the percentage of the total gross collections as set forth in Paragraph 4 above, from its distribution of the picture during the preceding week. Time and prompt payments are the essence of This Agreement.

a. **GROSS COLLECTIONS**: Gross Collections to Licensee for rental or use of said picture are defined as follows:

i)   The entire amount received for flat rentals; and

ii)   The entire amount paid by the theatre to which the pictures are rented on percentage.

8. **RECORDS**: Licensee shall keep and maintain, at its principal place of business, until the expiration or earlier termination of Licensee's rights or license hereunder, and for a period of three (3) years thereafter, complete detailed, permanent, true and accurate books of account and records relating to the distribution, exhibition and exploitation of the motion picture, including but without being limited to detailed box office receipts, detailed bookings thereof, rentals received and/or due and to grow due therefrom, gross collections derived therefor, detailed billings thereon, and detailed playdates thereof, whereabouts of prints, trailers, accessories and other material in connection with the motion picture. Licensee further agrees that all such books of account shall be approved by Licensor, and Licensee further agrees to give to Licensor or its accredited representative, until the expiration or earlier termination of Licensee's rights and license hereunder, and for a period of three (3) years thereafter, access at any time to the bookings, rentals and receipts derived from the exhibition, distribution and exploitation of the motion picture, and to permit Licensor or its representatives, during such time, to make extracts therefrom.

9. **RESERVATION OF RIGHTS**: Licensee acknowledges

that there is not granted to it under This Agreement any right in television, radio, 16mm, or any sub-standard sizes. All reproduction, remake, dramatic, pictorial, scenario, dialogue, literary and music rights, without any limitation whatever, are reserved to Licensor. No rights in non-theatrical exhibition are granted under This Agreement, except as set forth in Paragraph 2 above.

10. **GENERAL CONDITIONS**: Delivery hereunder shall mean delivery to a common carrier.

Licensor guarantees to withhold the showing of this picture on television for a period of _____.

Licensee agrees to order a minimum of _____ prints, and pay for same, including charges with the signing of This Agreement, and balance of prints to be ordered and paid for with order, and agrees to put the picture into release and distribution not later than sixty (60) days after receipt of first print.

The legal ownership of the prints delivered to Licensee, in accordance with Paragraph 4 above, shall remain with Licensor at all times, and at the expiration of the term of This Agreement, Licensee shall, at Licensor's request either destroy or return these prints to Licensor at Licensor's expense. If destroyed, Affidavit of Destruction, sworn to before a Notary Public, shall be furnished Licensor by Licensee.

Licensee further agrees to submit all contracts on all first-run-bookings for Licensor's approval, and at no time will such a contract be a binding contract with the exhibitor unless it has the signature of approval by an officer or a properly designated official of the Licensor. Licensee shall have the right to approve all subsequent-run bookings, and what is commonly known in the industry as spot-booking contracts.

Licensor will ship to, and Licensee will accept and pay for Press Books on the motion picture licensed, at $.25 each, F.O.B. Los Angeles, California.

Nothing herein contained shall be construed as constituting a joint venture or partnership between the parties hereto, and neither party shall have the authority to bind the other as its representative in any manner whatsoever, unless otherwise expressly provided in This Agreement.

If any provision of This Agreement shall be declared unenforceable, it shall be deemed deleted and shall not affect the enforceability of the remainder of This Agreement.

IN WITNESS WHEREOF, the parties to This Agreement have set their hands the day and year first above written.

_____

BY: _____

_____

BY: _____

CHAPTER 21

FRANCHISE SALES AGREEMENT

THIS AGREEMENT, made this _____ day of _____ 19 ____ , by and between _____ RELEASING CO., having its principal office at _____ Hollywood, CA 90028, (hereinafter referred to as "Licensor"), and _____ having its principal office at _____ (hereinafter referred to as "Licensee").

WITNESSETH:

For and in consideration of the mutual covenants contained herein, it is hereby agreed by and between the parties as follows:

1. **GRANT OF LICENSE:** Subject to the terms of this agreement, Licensor hereby grants licensee and licensee hereby accepts the sole and exclusive right, license and privilege to distribute, exploit and arrange for the exhibition of the motion pictures hereinafter described (hereinafter referred to as "the pictures"), for the theatrical exhibition only, in the territory hereinafter defined, for a license period hereinafter defined, or for such lesser period as Licensor may own the exclusive distribution, exhibition and exploitation rights thereto.

   a. **THE PICTURES**
   _____
   _____
   _____
   etc.

Licensee agrees to accept and actively distribute and exploit in good faith the pictures delivered and to be delivered to it hereunder and to use its best efforts to obtain the widest exhibition thereof possible at the highest rentals and license fees consistent with good business practice and judgment, and to the end that the greatest possible revenue shall be delivered by licensee and licensor from the pictures in the licensed territory.

2. **TERM:** The term of this agreement and the franchise

herein granted shall be for a period of twelve (12) months from the date of the exhibition of this agreement.

3. **TERRITORY**: The territory covered by this agreement and the theatrical license herein granted shall consist only of the territory specifically set forth hereinafter. The high seas, all inland waterways and all ships, railroads, airplanes and other common carriers are excluded from and shall be deemed to be outside the licensed territory. For the purpose of this agreement, the words "the territory" shall be construed to mean and refer to the territory hereinafter described. No rights of any kind or nature with respect to pictures outside the said territory are granted to or shall be exercised by Licensee, all such rights being reserved to Licensor.

TERRITORY: _____

_____

_____

4. **DELIVERY OF THE PICTURES**: During the term of this agreement, Licensor shall use its best efforts to deliver to Licensee prints of those pictures which Licensor is then releasing, and shall likewise use its best efforts to furnish to Licensee a sufficient number of 35mm prints to satisfy the requirements of Licensee.

5. **LIMITATION OF RIGHTS GRANTED LICENSEE;**
a. **35mm Theatrical Uses:** The license herein granted regarding all pictures hereunder is and shall be limited to the distribution, exhibition and exploitation, in the territory, of 35mm prints of the pictures in theatres or other auditorium regularly used for the commercial exhibition of motion pictures to the general public for an admission fee.

b. **Sub-Standard, Non-Theatrical Uses:** It is specifically understood and agreed that no rights are granted to or shall be exercised by Licensee with respect to 16mm, 8mm or other sub-standard gauge prints of the pictures or with respect to non-theatrical or non-commercial uses of the pictures in either standard widths except as provided in subdivision (g) below.

c. **Radio and Television Rights:** Licensor expressly reserves to itself all rights to broadcast or telecast the pictures or any part of any of them by means of radio or television transmission or by any other means or device now known or hereafter invented or discovered.

   d. **Literary, Dramatic and Musical Material:** Licensor expressly reserves to itself all rights whatsoever in the literary, dramatic, musical and other material used in or in connection with the pictures or in connection with the pictures or any of them. Nothing contained in this agreement shall be deemed to prevent or restrict Licensor from selling, using or otherwise dealing with all or any part of the said literary, dramatic, musical or other material in any manner, version, form or medium whatsoever; and Licensee shall have no right or interest therein or in the proceeds derived by Licensor therefrom.

   e. **General Reservation of Rights:** All rights in and to the pictures or in connection therewith which are not herein expressly granted and conveyed to Licensee are hereby reserved to Licensor.

   f. **Recognition of Licensor's Rights:** Licensee hereby expressly concedes, admits and recognizes, for all purposes, the copyrights and ownership in licensor of each and all of the pictures, all distribution, exhibition and exploitation rights therein or whatsoever kind and nature and all rights incident thereto, all literary, dramatic and musical material contained therein or upon which the pictures or any of them are based and all rights incident thereto, all physical properties appurtenant to the pictures or any of them, and the names and trademarks of Licensor, Licensee expressly agrees that it will not, for any purpose whatsoever, or under any circumstance whatsoever, or at anytime, contest, deny or dispute such ownership or the part of Licensor or recognize, admit or concede any conflicting rights in any party other than Licensor.

   g. **Army Camps:** Anything in this Paragraph 5 to the contrary notwithstanding, both Licensor and Licensee shall have the right to distribute and arrange for the exhibition of the pictures in United States Army, Navy, Marine Corps and Air Force camps located within the above described territory, whether or not such exhibitions shall be in theatres or auditorium regularly used for the exhibition of motion pictures and whether or not admission fees shall be charged therefor; provided, however, that the written approval of Licensor shall first be obtained for each such exhibition and that the same shall be subject to all of the other terms, covenants, conditions, limitations and provisions in this agreement contained. Distribution fees resulting from such playdates, all as more particularly set forth hereinafter.

6. EXHIBITION CONTRACTS:

a. **Forms:** All contracts for the exhibition of the pictures or any of them shall be entered into in the name of Licensor on forms furnished or approved in writing by Licensor.

b. **Approval by Licensor:** No application signed by an Exhibitor or theatre operator and countersigned by Licensee or its representative shall be or become a valid and binding contract for the exhibition of the pictures or any of them unless and until the same shall have been approved in writing by an authorized officer of Licensor at its home office.

c. **Separate Recognitions:** The motion pictures released by Licensor and delivered to Licensee hereunder shall be distributed, exploited, advertised, licensed, booked and otherwise dealt with by Licensee independently and apart from any other motion pictures which Licensor has granted or may hereafter grant permission to Licensee to distribute. In negotiating with exhibitors or theatre operators for the exhibition of Licensor's pictures, neither such negotiations nor dealings nor the terms of any agreement of proposed agreement in connection therewith shall be made conditional upon or shall be affected or influenced by the distribution, exhibition, exploitation, advertising, licensing, booking of, or other dealings pertaining to other motion pictures.

d. **Adjustments:** Licensee shall have no right or authority to cancel, revise, alter, adjust or otherwise amend any exhibition contracts for Licensor's pictures, nor shall Licensee permit, allow or grant any rebate, refunds, allowances or credits to any exhibitor, without the consent of Licensor in writing first obtained.

e. **General Obligations of Licensee:** It is of the essence of this agreement that Licensee shall not take any steps or permit or allow any acts or in any way deal with the pictures in any manner which may prevent or prejudice the derivation of the largest possible revenue from the distribution of the pictures in the licensed territory.

7. PRINTS, ACCESSORIES AND CENSORSHIP:

a. Licensor agrees to make available to Licensee, at Licensee's place of business, a normal requirement of press books and other advertising accessories.

b. **Title to Remain in Licensor:** Title in and to the pictures and all prints thereof and all advertising material and accessories pertaining thereto is and at all times shall be and remain vested in Licensor, its successors or assigns, and neither Licensee nor any exhibitor nor any person, form or corporation claiming from or through Licensee shall have any right, title or interest therein.

c. **Care of Prints:** Licensee agrees that at all times it will keep and maintain all the prints of the pictures delivered hereunder in good condition, suitable for proper and satisfactory exhibition except for ordinary wear and tear. All prints of the pictures or any parts thereof which may become damaged, worn or otherwise unsuitable for proper and satisfactory exhibition, shall be returned to Licensor or disposed of as Licensor may instruct.

d. **Covenant Against Duping:** Licensee covenants and agrees that it will not cause, suffer or permit the duplication, duping, reproduction or copying of the pictures or any part thereof, either directly or indirectly, or through any subsidiary, parent or affiliated corporations or any of it or their officers, directors, stockholder, agents, representatives or personnel.

Licensee covenants and agrees that it will promptly notify Licensor if, as and when Licensee receives knowledge or notice that any prints of the pictures or any part thereof has been or is about to be duplicated, reproduced or copied without the permission of Licensor.

e. **Loss, Theft or Destruction of Prints:** Licensee covenants and agrees that it will immediately notify Licensor of any loss, theft or destruction of prints, or any part thereof, licensed by Licensor hereunder, and will furnish an affidavit satisfactory to Licensor setting forth the facts of such loss, theft or destruction. Licensee covenants and agrees that it will use its best efforts, at its sole expense, to recover possession of any prints which may have been lost or stolen.

f. **Return of Prints:** Immediately upon the expiration of the distribution period for each of the pictures, or immediately upon the earlier termination of Licensee's rights hereunder, Licensee agrees that it will absolutely and unconditionally return to Licensor, or its designee, all prints under or in the possession or control of Licensee, and subsidiary, parent or affiliated corporations, and its or their officers, directors, stockholders, agents, employees, representatives or personnel, unless such prints have been lost, stolen or destroyed. The said prints shall be in as good condition as the same were when delivered to Licensee, excepting reasonable wear and tear incurred in the ordinary operation of Licensee's business.

g. **Alteration of Prints**: Licensee covenants and agrees that it will not cause, suffer or permit the prints, advertising material or accessories delivered hereunder to be changed, revised or altered in any manner whatsoever without the written consent of Licensor first obtained.

h. **Censorship**: If the laws prevailing in the licensed territory or any part thereof requires the approval of censor boards or other duly constituted officials or semi-officials authorities (hereinafter referred to as "censor boards") for the exhibition of motion pictures, Licensee agrees to apply for such approval or permission prior to the release of each of the pictures in the said territory.

In the event that any motion picture delivered by Licensor hereunder cannot be exhibited in any part of the licensed territory because such approval or permission has been refused by a local censor board, Licensee shall immediately send to Licensor a statement of all of the facts in connection therewith, together with a copy of the notice of refusal and rejection by such censor board, the reasons therefore, and all other communications to and from such censors in connection therewith. Licensor shall thereupon have the right, but not the duty, to cut or alter scenes or make elimination from or additions to the motion picture to meet the requirements of the censor board. In the event that Licensor elects to make such changes, Licensee agrees to re-submit the motion picture to the censor board and to cooperate in taking all necessary action to obtain the approval of the censor board.

i. **Cooperative Advertising**: Licensee agrees that it will not enter into any contracts or agreements, under the terms of which Licensor shall be committed to any form of financial obligation, including but not limited to contracts with any exhibitor for the exhibition of any of the pictures delivered herein, which contract or agreement provides for any advertising costs relating to the exhibition of motion pictures which is to be paid for in whole or in part by Licensor, wihtout first having had the consent in writing of Licensor. If Licensor approves such contracts or agreements, the method of recouping the cost of such "cooperative advertising" from the gross receipts of the picture or pictures so exhibited is set forth hereinafter.

8. GROSS RECEIPTS AND ALLOCATION THEREOF:

a. **Definition of Gross Receipts:** All exhibitors who have exhibited Licensor's picture shall be involved in the name of Licensor, on forms furnished to Licensee by Licensor, and all checks in payment thereof by the exhibitor shall be made payable in the name of Licensor and remitted directly to Licensor. For the purpose of this agreement, the term "gross receipts" shall be deemed to mean the entire proceeds, without any deductions whatsoever, paid to Licensor for the right to exhibit the pictures, or any of them, whether such license fees be paid on a flat rental basis or whether they be calculated on a percentage of exhibitor's receipts.

b. **Definition of Adjusted Gross Receipts:** For the purpose of this agreement, the term "adjusted gross receipts" shall be deemed to mean the entire proceeds received by Licensor from the exhibitor after an amount has been deducted therefrom.

c. **Distribution Fees:** Licensor shall forthwith pay to the Licensee, as and for Licensee's distribution fee, a sum equivalent to _____ percent of the adjusted gross receipts with respect to each of the pictures.

TERMS: _____

ALL ENGAGEMENTS IN LICENSED TERRITORY.

If a picture plays on a military base, as defined in sub-division (g) of Paragraph 5, the distribution fees payable to licensee shall be as follows: If the exhibition contract was arranged by Licensor, Licensee shall receive a sum equivalent to _____ percent of the gross receipts received and collected by the licensor for such playdates. If the exhibition contract was arranged by Licensee, Licensee shall receive a sum equivalent to _____ percent of the gross receipts received and collected by the Licensor for such playdates.

d. **Miscellaneous:** If an exhibitor remits any receipts directly to Licensee, Licensee hereby agrees to endorse said check (if same is made payable to Licensee) and to transmit said check in kind directly to Licensor. If said check contains funds not belonging to Licensor, Licensor agrees to immediately transmit to Licensee its check for those funds, allowing sufficient time for the exhibitor's check to clear. Licensee agrees to act as trustee for Licensor on any such receipts which are remitted to it, and Licensee hereby assigns to Licensor all of the Licensee's right, title and interest in and to such receipts.

9. **REPORTS:** During the term of this agreement, Licensee will furnish a statement, not later than Friday of each week, indicating the following:

a. Written statements, on forms furnished to Licensee by Licensor, indicating all transactions had by Licensee with respect to the pictures during the immediately preceding calendar week;

b. Copies of all exhibition arrangements for approval and consent in writing by Licensor.

c. Duplicate copies of all final agreements consumated with exhibitors or theatre operators with respect to the pictures.

d. Duplicate copies of box office reports received from exhibitors immediately following playdates of the pictures.

e. Duplicate copes of all tearsheets (advertising) and invoices covering such advertising.

10. **BOOKS AND REPORTS:** Licensee shall keep and maintain, at its principal place of business, until the expiration or earlier termination of Licensee's rights or license hereunder, and for a period of four (4) years thereafter, complete, detailed, permanent, true and accurate books of account and records relating to the distribution, exhibition and exploitation of each of the pictures, including but without being limited to, detailed box office receipts, detailed bookings thereof, rentals received and/or due and to become due therefrom, gross receipts derived therefrom, detailed billings thereon and detailed play-dates thereof, whereabouts of prints, trailers, accessories and other material in connection with the pictures. Licensee further agrees that all such books of account and records shall be kept and maintained under a standard system, and according to methods approved in writing by Licensor, or its accredited representative, until the expiration or earlier termination of Licensee's right and license hereunder, and for a period of four (4) years thereafter, access at any time to all of the books, accounts, records, papers and vouchers of Licensee

pertaining to the booking, rentals, and receipts derived from the exhibition, distribution and exploitation of the pictures and to permit Licensor or its representatives during such time to make extracts therefrom.

13. **CREDITS**: Licensee agrees to observe all of Licensor's obligations with respect to credits and advertising for the pictures, all in accordance with the advertising material furnished Licensee and the credits appearing on each picture itself.

14. **DEFAULT BY LICENSEE**: If Licensee shall breach or become in default of performance of any material term or provision of this agreement, and fail to cure same within thirty (30) days after receipt of written notice specifying same or if Licensee (a) shall be adjudicated a bankrupt, or (b) make an assignment for the benefit of creditors, or (c) if Licensee shall abandon its present business, or (d) if Licensee shall petition for or consent to any relief under any bankruptcy, receivership, reorganization, liquidation or arrangement statutes, then and in any of said events, Licensor shall have the right to terminate this agreement in addition to other rights and remedies at law. Upon such termination, all bonafide contracts theretofore entered into between Licensee and any exhibitor or sub-licensee shall be automatically assigned to Licensor. Licensor shall be entitled to immediate possession of all prints of the pictures, advertising materials and all other materials pertaining to the pictures, and Licensee agrees to deliver possession thereof to such place as Licensor may designate.

Licensee agrees to execute any and all assignments and other instruments deemed by Licensor to be reasonably necessary to evidence such assignment of exhibition contracts, and Licensee agrees to turn over to Licensor all records, including books, billing and delivery records, pertaining to the pictures and all monies on hand to which Licensor is then entitled.

15. **GENERAL PROVISIONS**:
   a. **No Partnership**: Nothing contained in this agreement shall be construed as constituting a joint venture or partnership between the parties hereto and neither party shall have the authority to bind the other as its representative in any manner

whatsoever unless otherwise so expressly provided in this agreement.

b. **No Representation as to Amount of Receipts:** Licensee has made no representations to Licensor regarding amount, extent or availability of gross receipts from the pictures.

c. **Use of Licensor's Forms:** Licensee agrees to use Licensor's contract forms in making exhibition arrangements.

d. **No Continuing Waiver:** The failure of Licensor on any occasion to enforce any provisions in this agreement shall not stop it from enforcing such provisions upon any other occasion or occasions if Licensor elects so to do and no waiver on the part of Licensor, express or implied, of any part of this agreement, shall be construed as a general or continuing waiver.

e. **Termination:** Either party may terminate this agreement by serving a thirty (30) day notice on the other in writing.

f. **Licensor's Approvals:** All playdates and/or requests for consent to participate in cooperative advertising must be submitted to Licensor a minimum of ten (10) days in advance of such playdate or use of such advertising, so as to give Licensor ample opportunity to either approve, amend or reject same.

g. **No Assignment:** The obligations and covenants of Licensee to be performed thereunder are personal and this agreement cannot be transferred, assigned, encumbered, pledged or otherwise hypothecated, in whole or in part, by Licensee either voluntarily or by operation of law, or otherwise, without the consent in writing of Licensor in each instance first had and obtained. The rights of Licensor hereunder may be assigned in whole or in part by Licensor and this agreement shall inure to the benefit of Licensor, its assignees and successors.

h. **Amendments:** No amendment, supplement or modification of this agreement shall be binding upon Licensor unless the same is in writing executed by duly authorized officers of Licensor. No representation, covenants, conditions or agreements exist between the parties other than those expressly set forth in writing herein.

i. **Time of Essence:** Time is hereby declared to be of the essence for the performance by Licensee of all the conditions, covenants and obligations on its part to be kept and performed.

j. **Violations Under Copyright Act:** It is of the essence

of this agreement that the exhibition by Licensee of any pictures covered hereby, after default by Licensee or in violation of the provisions of this agreement, shall be deemed an unauthorized exhibition by Licensee in violation of the copyright act. It is further agreed that any exhibition for which payment has not been made to Licensor, as herein provided, shall likewise be deemed an exhibition in violation of the copyright act; it being the intention hereof that any exhibition of any such picture in violation of the provisions of this agreement, or without payment therefore, as provided in this agreement, shall be deemed an infringement of copyrights in connection with.said picture.

IN WITNESS WHEREOF, the parties to this agreement have set their hands the day and year first above written.

RELEASING CO.

by_____
   ("Licensor")

by_____
   ("Licensee")

CHAPTER 22

MAJOR DISTRIBUTORS

The "major" distributors include:

Paramount
Warner
United Artists
Universal
Twentieth Century Fox
Columbia
Allied Artists
American International
Buena Vista (Walt Disney)

Former "major" distributors which left the distribution business include:

MGM
RKO
Republic

Major distributors may (a) produce movies, (b) finance movies, (c) own studio and/or locations, (d) distribute pictures acquired from others.

Various distribution companies may from time to time be more active in distribution then the companies listed above.

CHAPTER 23

NATO – NATIONAL ASSOCIATION OF THEATRE OWNERS

There are lots of little regional NATOs, and there is the national NATO.

NATO's complaints arc generally directed against distributors' practices such as blind bidding and rough terms.

When exhibitors refused to book pictures on terms deemed liveable by certain distributors, the distributors offered to go into the exhibition business by renting theatres for one week at a time, or for slightly longer periods. This is known as the Four-Wall method. It allows the exhibitor to forego the risk of exhibiting, and forces the distributor to assume the gambles of distribution and exhibition.

The exhibitors liked the Four-Wall scheme, at least for a while. Part of the distribution Four-Wall concept calls for a tremendous amount of advertising to pull into the theatre a tremendous amount of people. The exhibitor enjoyed being paid enough to make a profit, getting people into his theatre, and all without any risk.

Then some major producer-distributors decided to Four-Wall major winners. The distributors paid willing exhibitors flat fees. But the distributors refused to pay any additional percentages based on box office plateaus.

Some Exhibitors who were quite willing to Four-Wall in order to avoid taking risks, were not willing to Four-Wall when there were no risks.

Other exhibitors foresaw that exhibitors might lose the opportunities to present pictures to smaller, less powerful theatres which were willing to Four-Wall a picture.

Thereupon some exhibitors made sounds to the effect that Four-Walling was illegal, violated the Consent Decree separating production and exhibition, and tried to have NATO take a position against Four-Walling.

NATO is so big, and there are so many people in regional NATOs, that it really is not difficult to find some NATO or former NATO official willing to take any stand on any position.

Whenever a position against distributor is (1) threatened, (2) discussed, (3) taken by NATO or NATO connected people, two threats are made:

1. The distributors will be sued for violating the anti-trust laws.

2. The Department of Justice will be asked to look into the situation.

NATO is powerful. Not all-powerful, but quite powerful.

INSTITUTE FOR ADULT EDUCATION

P.O. BOX 2710 / HOLLYWOOD, CALIF. 90028 / (213) 461-3811

CIRCUIT	THEATRE	TOWN and STATE	PICTUR

RECOMMENDATIONS:

INSTRUCTIONS: PREPARE IN TRIPLICATE. FORWARD TWO COPIES TO
INSTITUTE DAILY FOR APPROVAL. RETAIN ONE COPY
FOR FOLLOW-UP. BILL FROM APPROVED COPY RE-
TURNED BY INSTITUTE

PLAYDATE WORK SHEET

WEEK BEGINNING_____

CONTRACT REC.	ADVANCE PAID	PLAYDATE	PRIOR DATE CANCELLED	RENTAL	REMARKS

BOOKER

FOR ADULT EDUCATION

CHAPTER 24

PLAYING WITH FIGURES

If a motion picture costs $20,000; and if the PRODUCER receives $20,000; then the PRODUCER may later make a profit.

If a motion picture costs $1,000,000; and if the PRODUCER receives only $20,000; then the PRODUCER has lost a lot of money.

Pictures of commercial theatrical length (72 minutes — 90 minutes) have been made for under $20,000; many of these have made a profit.

Pictures of the same length have been made for over $1,000,000; many of these have lost money.

Query — Why does anyone make very expensive pictures?

Answer — Because more expensive pictures have better box office potential than less expensive pictures.

Answer — Because bigger budgets mean bigger salaries for producers.

CHAPTER 25

POPCORN; CONCESSIONS, PASSES

Exhibitors may own and operate their own concessions, or they may license (for flat fee or percentage or both) concessions (parking, candy counter, vending machines) to third parties.

An exhibitor may allow customers to see the movies without paying anything for tickets (e.g., free passes) for reasons benefiting the exhibitor, but not benefiting the motion picture's distributor or producer.

A chain may collect money selling passes to senior citizens, students, or other groups.

Distributors contend that all these amounts received by the exhibitors are received only because distributors furnish movies, and that distributors should share in the proceeds.

The extent of such sharing is negotiable.

Producers should remember that they should place into the producer-distributor contract provisions enabling them to share in such proceeds with the distributor.

CHAPTER 26

PORNOGRAPHY

Pornographic films include those which receive X ratings and many films which are not submitted for rating classification.

There are a few multi-million dollar box office pornographic films. Generally, the box office is much lower because (1) the number of theatres is relatively small and (2) the regular audience for pornographic films is relatively small.

X-rated films are sometimes hounded by prurient people and police. These hounders may bother the producer, the distributor and/or the exhibitor.

The hounders follow an economic theory of warfare; by picketing, arrests, trials, jail, and other threats and acts, the hounders cause x-rated film producers, distributors, and exhibitors to spend their **time** anticipating and countering threats and their **money** paying bailbondsmen, lawyers, cops, and politicians. This economic warfare is designed to ruin x-rated producers and to drive them out of business.

X-rated producers have counter-attacked legally and economically by insisting on trials, appeals, rehearings. Police and district attorneys habitually complain that they are under-staffed and overworked. It is more economical for police and district attorneys to bust 100 prostitutes and bookmakers who quickly plead guilty and pay small fines, than to spend the same time trying to catch and convict a single well-heeled x-rated producer.

Pornography has so changed in meaning that the term itself often no longer means that a pornographic film violates any law. There is soft core pornography and hard core pornography.

There is no one nationwide test as to what is pornographic; each political judge and square jury can decide for himself whether a movie is pornographic. This has led to prosecution after prosecution of the same film in different communities even though in all previous trials concerning the film the defendant was found "Not Guilty."

The normal Producer-Distributor contract contains a warranty by the Producer that the picture is not obscene, and a general promise that the Producer will pay damages if any warranty is incorrect. The normal Distributor-Exhibitor contract contains a similar provision.

When an Exhibitor is hounded, the hounders have followed various tactics.

In Manhattan, projectionists have been arrested, jailed, and released the next day. This warfare by "kidnaping" was resisted by the projectionists' union, and the "kidnapings" stopped.

In Los Angeles, cashiers have been arrested, and the costs of the bail, attorney, and $100 fines paid by theatres. Theatres deduct such costs from the amounts payable by the Exhibitors to the Distributors. Nobody was hurt badly except the poor working cashiers who would lose their jobs and have criminal records for the rest of their lives.

In little towns throughout the United States, theatres switched from playing G and GP pictures for empty houses to playing X pictures to filled houses; the theatre owners were able to increase charitable contributions and political contributions, and have been generally left alone.

The Supreme Court's June 1973 decisions concerning pornography passed the job of deciding what is and is not criminally pornographic to localities.

Some distributors became scared of potential legal expenses, left off distributing X pictures, and distributed R-rated pictures.

Other producers, distributors and exhibitors decided that

costs of bail, attorneys and fines were normal business expenses, and switched from soft core pornography to hard core pornography.

So many prosecutors had heard about the bad economic results on prosecutors' offices caused by prosecuting accused pornographers, that most prosecutors decided to not bother local exhibitors playing pornographic pictures.

Since generally neither hard core nor soft core pornographic pictures were prosecuted, and hard core pictures frequently had better box office receipts than soft core pictures, the market for soft core pictures declined.

Few theatres played soft core pictures; the flat fees paid by exhibitors for soft core pictures decreased; inflation entered into the picture, costs of air freight and other distribution expenses increased.

Several distributors of soft core pictures went out of business. Producers of pictures handled by these distributors wanted their pictures back. Distributors returned pictures only upon the producers waiving rights to all money due to the producers.

The men who exhibit pictures and have the nerve to flout the community's prurient people, also have the nerve to cheat distributors. The men who distribute pictures and have the nerve to risk prosecution in 50 states, also have the nerve to cheat producers.

The method of cheating is simple; slow pay, low pay, no pay.

The money owners **pay slowly, pay less** than is agreed to (by claiming they paid attorneys' fees and pay-offs and by keeping reserves for later attorneys' fees), and sometimes simply don't pay at all.

The men to whom money is owed hesitate to use the courts to sue. A judge who hears such a case may recommend that all parties involved in the civil case be criminally prosecuted for pornography.

CHAPTER 27

THE PREVIEW AND THE TEST SHOWING

Producers use previews to test audience reaction during the period producers are still tinkering with pictures.

Distributors use previews to learn whether they should tinker with the pictures, how the preview audience likes the picture, what should be stressed in advertising the picture.

Exhibitors use previews to hype up the box office when the current attraction is not doing well.

A distributor may test the picture in various ways.

For example, he may approach an exhibitor who has a theatre in a city which has served reliably in past tests.

The exhibitor and distributor may test an advertising campaign by concept and budget. The concept may be similar and the budget may be close to those of previously tested films.

The box office receipts are analyzed closely, by type of tickets, times of day, days of week. These results are compared with previous tests.

Search is made for the results of advertising. Did the current picture outdraw the former test pictures on Wednesday, Friday, Saturday, Sunday?

Search is made for the results of reviews. Are reviews published on Thursdays? Did the current picture outdraw the former test pictures on Thursday?

Search is made for the results of word-of-mouth. Did the current picture outdraw the former test picture on Sunday, Monday, Tuesday and weeks after the first?

If word-of-mouth is good, then it may be worthwhile to have a picture play in just one theatre for a while. Only after word-of-mouth has done its work, should the picture go into multiple.

If the picture has a well-known star, but word-of-mouth is poor, then the picture might net most by being shown in multiples, but not in as many multiples as a better picture.

Tests should consider other factors which may influence results. For example, audiences may be better the week after unemployment and welfare checks are issued than the second week after such payments. Competition from a county fair, travelling circus or rodeo, etc. may kill the box office of whatever movie might be playing the theatre during the test week.

CHAPTER 28

PRINTS

If a 35mm color print for a 90 minute picture costs about $700, calculate the cost of the prints you may require.

10 prints times $700 per print equals $7000. (A very low budget x-rated picture may be distributed with 10 prints.)

40 prints times $700 per print equals $28000. (A low budget quickie exploitation picture may be distributed with 40 prints.)

200 prints times $700 per print equals $140,000. (A high budget picture may be distributed with 200 prints.)

Be careful of each of these figures. A picture may run longer or less than 90 minutes; the longer the picture, the higher the costs of each print.

Be careful of the cost per print used above, the $700. Prints may cost more or less.

Be careful of the exact number of prints used above. Each type of distribution (low budget X, low budget exploitation, high budget) tries to tailor-order the number of prints to the specific picture.

CHAPTER 29

PRINTS AND
ADVERTISING AND
INTEREST

Advertising is expensive.

If the same advertising can bring audiences to two non-competing theatres, then the cost of advertising per theatre is cut in half.

The same theory holds good for 10 theatres and for 40 theatres. Therefore distributors may want multiple runs in as many theatres as practical for the film.

Few porn films have multiple runs in as many as 10 theatres. Since each theatre which runs the film on the same dates as other theatres, only 10 prints may be needed to cover the major market of a territory.

But exploitation films may be good for multiple runs in up to 40 theatres in a territory. Therefore, 40 prints may be needed.

The advertising territory for a big film may be national. The stars may plug the film on national television programs. Advertisements may appear in national magazines. The same company which distributes the film may have borrowed money to produce it; therefore it may be interested in paying back the loan as quickly as possible. Therefore, 200 prints may be needed.

Advertising in a metropolitan area may cost $5000 — $50,000 for a campaign. A small distributor may be financially rich enough to handle one campaign a month; therefore he may only need 40 prints for one campaign.

A major distributor may be rich enough to handle campaigns in several metropolitan areas at once. Therefore he can use 200 prints.

CHAPTER 30

PRODUCER – DISTRIBUTOR CONTRACT

1. Granting clause. Producer gives Distributor the right to distribute the picture.

2. Territory clause. The territory for which Distributor is given rights is _____ (for example, (a) U.S. and Canada, or (b) Western Hemisphere except U.S. and Canada, or (c) Europe except U.S.S.R., or (d) planet Earth, or . . .)

3. Duration. For example: (a) 10 years, (b) Forever, (c) One year with automatic renewal for each following year if during current year Distributor has paid at least $ _____ to Producer.

4. Calculation of Distributor Payments To or For Producer.

5. Delivery date

6. Warranties. (a) Copyright. (b) No Defamation or Obscenity or Piracy. (c) No outstanding liens, debts.

7. Non-theatrical operations. Promise of no television showings for two years or other period of time.

8. Other provisions.

9. Identification of parties

10. Identification of motion picture (Title, producer, director, stars, required credits).

CHAPTER 31

THE PRODUCER
GIVES MONEY AWAY

The producer tries to raise money and use credit in order to be able to produce a picture.

Money sources include:
    (a)   The producer's own savings.
    (b)   Money from partners.
    (c)   Money from investors.
    (d)   Money from lenders

Credit sources include:
    (a)   Persons who render services on credit; when insiders such as writers, actors, directors do so, these are called deferrals.
    (b)   Suppliers who furnish supplies on credit; camera and sound equipment may be borrowed by producers with good credit.
    (c)   Movie Laboratories.
    (d)   Banks
    (e)   Investors who may wish to hedge their bet by providing some money as interest bearing loans (and the rest as acquirers of limited partner interests or shares of stock).
    (f)   Loan guarantors.
    (g)   Unwilling creditors, who thought they would be paid, but were not.

The creditors may wish to be protected from the producer's possible misusing funds the producer may receive from the distributors. Creditors may insist that they be paid directly by the distributor. (Note: This may allow the distributor to misuse the funds.)

The distributor may calculate that he owes money to the production company. For example, the distributor may owe $200,000 to the production company. But before paying the production company, the distributor will pay (since the producer-distributor contract so provides):

(a)	Bank loan	$100,000	unpaid principal.
		21,000	10% interest for two years compounded annually.
(b)	Movie lab	$ 50,000	production costs and prints; interest
(c)	Suppliers	$ 20,000	principal; interest.
(d)	Unwilling creditors	$ 20,000	(These may be payroll taxes withheld from employees but illegally not paid to the Internal Revenue Service; interest.)
(e)	Fee to loan guarantors	$ 2,000	
(f)	Deferrals to writer, actors, others	$ 77,000	
	TOTAL TO CREDITORS	$300,000.	

Therefore, since the $300,000 is paid to the Producer's creditors, etc., the Producer will receive for himself a grand total of $0.00.

CHAPTER 32

PRODUCER SEES DISTRIBUTOR

FIRST VISIT

Producer: I am going to produce a motion picture tentatively entitled RETURN OF THE SON OF FRANKENSTEIN.

Distributor: Good idea. Do you have a script?

Producer: I have a treatment and a first draft of a screenplay. The writer and I are working on the script.

Distributor: Let me see it when it's finished. Who's your director?

Producer: Able Baker. He's directed no movies, but has directed lots of television.

Distributor: (1) That's good. He knows how to get a lot of product in the can each day. (2) That's bad. Television directors have 3 basic shots (medium, close-up, extreme close-up). Movies need long shots and various shots. Television budgets, after paying for expensive sets and high union salaries, frequently have little money left for the constant moving action that movies need. A television director may not be able to make a low budget movie move enough.

Producer: Lots of television directors have made it big in movies. Here are some reviews of Able Baker's shows.

Distributor: Who are your stars? I'll be happy to distribute any picture you make if it stars Steve McQueen.

Producer: My story does not need hot name stars. I have talked with these well-known actors, and they have tentatively agreed that they will be available for the amounts I show on the budget.

Distributor: How are you going to finance your picture?

Producer: I was hoping you would.

Distributor: I won't. I put my money into distribution.

Producer: I have talked to a bank; bank loan guarantors; the actors and director will defer parts of their salaries; the lab is willing to work on credit; I have some investors. But everyone insists that the distributor make guarantees.

Distributor: I won't guarantee any payments. I am willing to agree to pay everyone out of the Producer's share of net film rentals.

Producer: How much do you pay Producers?

Distributor: You have three choices. First choice: Distributor pays for Prints and Ads. Second choice: Distributor advances money for Producer to pay for Prints and Ads. Third choice: Producer comes up with money to pay for Prints and Ads.

Producer: What if I select the first choice?

Distributor: We split: 65% for me. 35% for you.

Producer: What if I select the second choice?

Distributor: We split 50% for me, 50% for you. I advance the funds for Prints and Ads, then reimburse myself out of your 50%.

Producer: What if I select the third choice?

Distributor: We split: 35% for me. 65% for you.

Producer: I talked with another distributor. You offered different percentages than he did.

Distributor: I am totally inconsistent from time to time. I am not bound to the terms I mention orally today. I'll only be bound when you and I sign a contract.

Producer: Are the terms you offered me standard terms?

Distributor: No. there are no standard terms.

DISTRIBUTOR TELEPHONES SUB-DISTRIBUTOR

Distributor: Hello, Jack. How are the kids?

Sub-Distributor: Barbara is pregnant and the boy does not want to marry her. Bobby is stoned all the time.

Distributor: How do you think a picture will do if it is called RETURN OF THE SON OF FRANKENSTEIN?

Sub-Distributor: Horror pictures have not been doing well for the past two years in this area. It may be time for them to do well again.

Distributor: When are you going to send me money for the multiple run you handled for my double feature: "BULLET EATING BABIES BATTLE TEENAGE BABY EATING BARBARIANS" and "RETURN OF YOUNG ADULTS."

Sub-Distributor: As soon as I collect from the Exhibitors. I would like to handle in my territory your current release entitled, "GOSH. GEE. OW. WOW."

Distributor: O.K. Get bookings.

SUB-DISTRIBUTOR TELEPHONES THEATER

Sub-Distributor: Hi. How's the family?

Exhibitor: Wife's fine. Joan's fine. If you are calling about your money for "BULLET EATING BABIES" and "RETURN OF YOUNG ADULTS," officially, I am waiting for my advertising bill from the radio station.

Sub-Distributor: When will your new twin theaters in the new shopping center open?

Exhibitor: Next month.

Sub-Distributor: I have the perfect picture for your opening. It's called "BOSH. GEE. OW. WOW."

Exhibitor: I can't tell by the title whether the picture is GP or X. Let me see your advertising material and how well the picture has done elsewhere.

Sub-Distributor: How well do you think a picture will do with a title "RETURN OF THE SON OF FRANKENSTEIN"?

Exhibitor: I have three theaters in which horror pictures will do well. If the campaign is right, I might add three more pictures to the multiple run.

CHAPTER 33

PRODUCERS, HOW TO
QUALIFY A DISTRIBUTOR

The word "producer" represents the individual who has persuaded a lot of people to go along with him. The word "producer" also means "production company."

There is a conflict between the individual and the production company. Thus a distributor may be acceptable to the individual, while the distributor is not necessarily acceptable to the production company. Unfortunately for the production company, the individual may put his own interests ahead of those of the production company.

The individual producer wants: (a) his salary for making the picture, (b) his share of profits.

If a producer is cynical or realistic enough to minimize the importance of (b) his share of profits, then one factor emerges as all-important: (a) his salary for making the picture.

The individual producer then only has one qualification for a distributor: (a) will the signing of a distribution contract enable the individual producer to collect his salary for making the picture?

If the distribution contract enables the producer to collect his salary, then all the other terms of the distribution contract may matter little to the individual producer.

This is one reason why many distribution contracts so favor the distributor.

A second qualification of the distributor is how likely he is able to pay to and for the producer enough money to enable (1) all creditors to be paid, (2) all backers and the producer to make healthy profits.

The following questions may be asked:

1. How long has the distributor been in business?
2. How powerful is the distributor?
3. Does the distributor have enough money and credit to properly obtain sufficient prints and sufficient advertising?
4. Does the distributor distribute the type of film which the producer wants to or has produced?
5. How well did the distributor pay the producers of the pictures distributed by the distributors during the last 3 years?
6. Would you buy a used car from this man?
7. What are the terms of the distribution contract?
8. Is the distributor trying to chisel the producer at the start by insisting that the legal fees of the distributor's lawyer for drafting the distribution contract be paid out of the picture's budget? (or out of producer's share of receipts?).

CHAPTER 34

PRODUCTION – DISTRIBUTION – EXHIBITION

This book appears elementary in many parts; the simplifications may be oversimplifications. This book may be current in part, current while it is written, which may cause it to be dated when it is read. This book may have other disadvantages; but it has one overwhelming advantage to readers: this book exists! It is very difficult for persons, both inside and outside the film distribution business to find text material on the distribution business.

Motion picture distribution is one part of a sequence of three parts. The three parts are 1. PRODUCTION. 2. DISTRIBUTION. 3. EXHIBITION.

These three parts are related.

The **producer** who is trying to package a picture can try to do so without trying to involve a distributor; the producer can package the script, director, performers, technical crew, financial backers and can produce the completed picture without trying to involve a distributor; but after the picture is completed, the producer faces the problem of distribution of the film to exhibitors.

The **distributor** needs product (motion pictures) to distribute. The distributor's job is to obtain money from exhibitors.

The **exhibitor** needs product (motion pictures) to exhibit to viewers. Exhibitors obtain product from distributors, who obtain product from producers.

Every once in a while this book may contain snide remarks about some group having the reputation of being suckers, dumb, sharp, crooked. Any such remarks are quite controversial.

Each of the three groups (production, distribution, exhibition) complains about the other two groups. Members of each group often complain about other members of the group.

Let us follow the flow of money.

The viewer pays cash at the theatre box office to the **exhibitor**.

The exhibitor is supposed to pay the **distributor** (in accordance with the exhibitor-distributor contract).

The distributor is supposed to pay the **producer** (in accordance with the distributor-producer contract).

Complaints follow the flow of product. The distributor complains about the producer's movie. The exhibitor complains about the distributor's movie.

Complaints follow the flow of money. Other complaints follow the absence of money. Exhibitors complain about too few box office customers. Distributors complain that Exhibitors pay too little and too late. Producers complain that Distributors pay too little and too late.

Why are there complaints about money? Are the low-slow paying parties crooked? Are the producers who sign a contract with distributors which allow for slow payments stupid, ignorant, and lazy?

For possible answers to these questions, read on.

-105-

Racket #4 (Continued)

Box Office.........$1200⁰⁰

Theater Share......$ 600⁰⁰

Sub-Distributor's Share.............$ 600⁰⁰

Sub-D's ½ of Advertising.........$250⁰⁰

Theater Pays $ 350⁰⁰ Sub-D

Newspaper Refund to Sub-D:

① The difference between national advertising and local rate..............$100⁰⁰

② 15% commission for getting business for newspaper-----$75⁰⁰

③ 2% cash discount...$12⁰⁰

Sub-Distributor Receives Refund....$187⁰⁰

RACKET # 4 (Continued)

SUMMARY:

Phoney Advertising Expenses Billed by Newspaper..... $600.00
Secret Refund to Exhibitor. $187.00
Actual Advertising Expense $413.00
Exhibitor SHOULD Pay 50% $206.50
Sub-Distributor SHOULD Pay 50% $206.50
Sub-Distributor DID Pay $250.00

SUB-DISTRIBUTOR
WAS CHEATED OUT OF $43.50

RACKET # 7

DISTRIBUTOR KEEPS A SECOND SET OF BOOKS FOR PRODUCER

PRODUCER

RECEIVED FROM SUB-DISTRIBUTOR $900⁰⁰

PRODUCER'S SHARE $600⁰⁰

DISTRIBUTOR

DISTRIBUTOR KEEPS A TRUE SET OF BOOKS FOR HIMSELF

RECEIVED FROM SUB-DISTRIBUTOR $1500⁰⁰

PRODUCER'S SHARE $1000⁰⁰

Summation of the Rackets:

	ACTUAL	EXHIBITOR LIES	SUB-D LIES	DISTRIBUTOR LIES
Box office receipts:...100%	$10,000	$6,000		
Due to Sub-Distributor:....50%	$5,000	$3,000	$2,000	
Due to Distributor:......37½%	$3,750	------	$1,500	$900.00
Due to Producer:......25%	$2,500	------	------	$600.00

RACKET..? OR BUSINESS..?

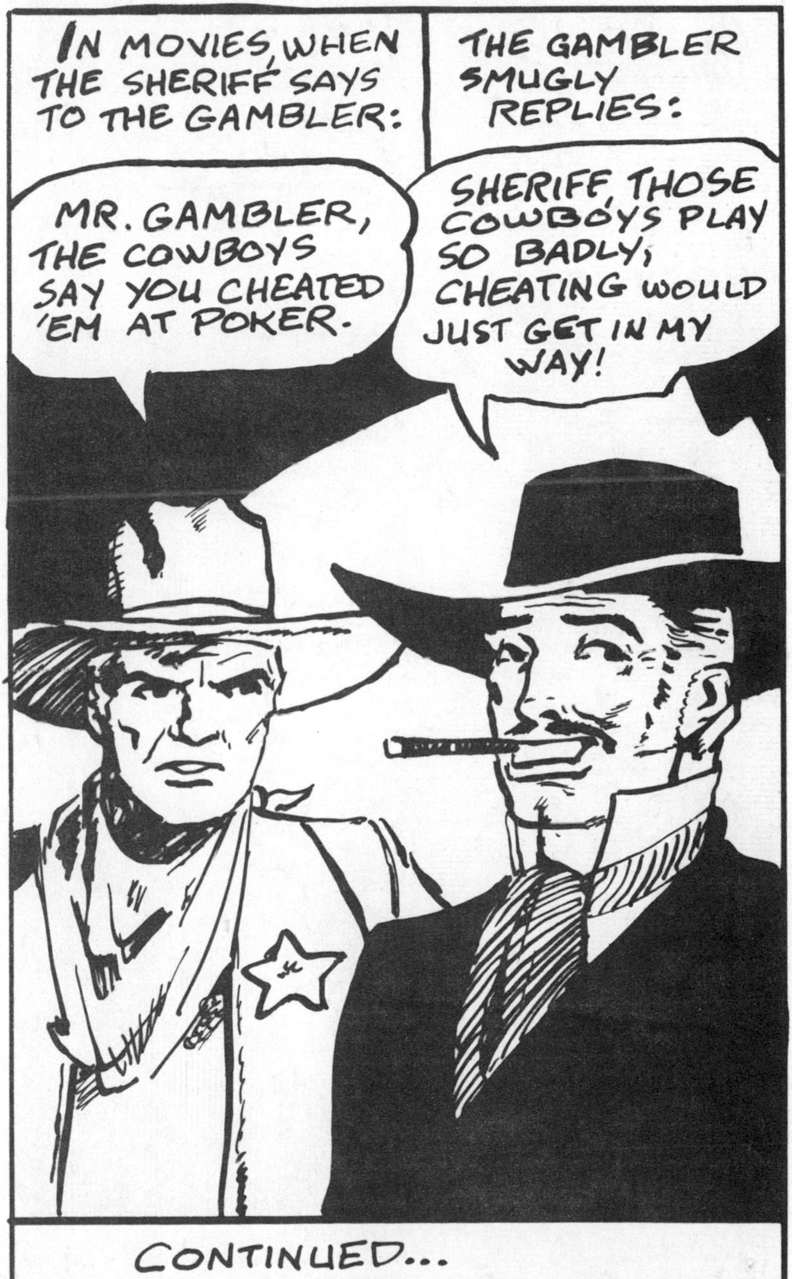

RACKET..? OR BUSINESS..? (CONT'D)

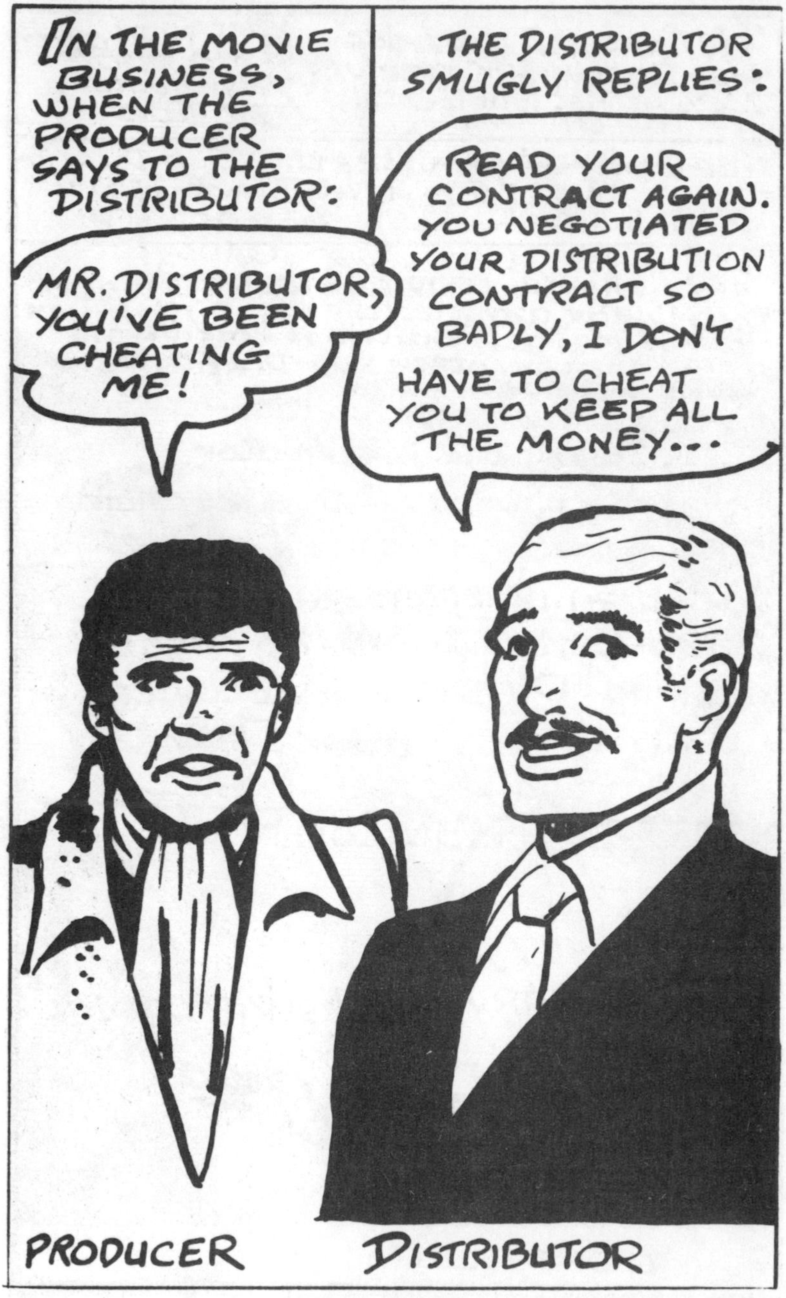

RACKET..? OR BUSINESS..?

The Contract provides that Distributor receives 25% of Net Film Rental.	Net Film Rental: $10,000. Distributor: $2,500

The Contract provides that Sub-Distributor receives 25% of Net Film Rental: $2,500

The Contract provides that if the Distributor handles the Sub-Distribution in an area, he is entitled to receive no more than any other Sub-Distributor would receive.

So... when the Distributor makes a phone call to a big chain in an area, and thus does not need an independent local Sub-Distributor, the phone-calling Distributor receives both the 25% for Distribution and the 25% for Sub-Distribution.

DISTRIBUTOR/SUB-DISTRIBUTOR:

$5000⁰⁰

RACKET..? OR BUSINESS..?

ITEM: PRODUCER PAYS PRODUCTION EXPENSES.

ITEM: DISTRIBUTOR **SAYS** HE HAS EXPENSES OF DISTRIBUTION SUCH AS ADVERTISING, PRINTS, FREIGHT, ETC.

ITEM: THE CONTRACT CLEARLY EXPRESSES THAT: "DISTRIBUTOR SHALL PAY COSTS OF ADVERTISING, PRINTS, FREIGHT, ETC."

ITEM: DO PRODUCERS AND LAWYERS UNDERSTAND ACCOUNTING LANGUAGE: "...WHICH SHALL BE DEBITED TO PRODUCER'S ACCOUNT"???

DO _YOU_ UNDERSTAND THIS LANGUAGE?

IT MEANS:

"IN THE LONG RUN, PRODUCERS SHALL PAY SUCH DISTRIBUTION EXPENSES AS ADVERTISING, PRINTS, FREIGHT, ETC."

SEE IT NOW "THE STRANGERS"

STARRING WINDA DLAKE

BIJOU

FILM

RACKET? OR BUSINESS? OR WHAT?

RACKET? BUSINESS? SCHEME?

+ THIS CONTRACT CAN BE MISLEADING.

SO... SUB-D. CORP. COLLECTS RENTAL FROM EXHIBITOR, PAYS IT OUT IN EXCESSIVE SALARY TO OWNER OF SUB.-D. CORP.... AND SUB-DISTRIBUTOR CORPORATION GOES BANKRUPT!

WHAT'S MY RACKET?

NOW...HEAR THIS ONE!

BIJOU · RON RICH RIDES · RON RICH RIDES · 6 P.M. SHOW · RON RICH RIDES

AFTER FILM IS SHOWN, IT IS TAKEN TO THE NEXT THEATER

The BROADWAY · RON RICH RIDES · 8 P.M. SHOW

...WHERE IT IS SHOWN TWO HOURS LATER...WITHOUT RENTAL BEING PAID!

EXHIBITOR RENTS FILM FOR SHOWING IN ONE THEATER (THE BIJOU), BUT SECRETLY, WITHOUT PAYING EXTRA RENTAL, SHOWS IT ALSO IN ANOTHER THEATER (THE BROADWAY) IN ANOTHER TOWN AT ANOTHER TIME!

HAVE ANOTHER VARIATION...

NOW...TWO FILMS ARE SWITCHED BETWEEN
TWO THEATERS...WITH RENTALS PAID FOR
ONLY ONE THEATER.

VARIATIONS: ANOTHER SHOWING COULD
BE ONE NOT ADVERTISED: AT A PRIVATE
OR SEMI-PRIVATE SCHOOL, FRATERNAL
ORGANIZATION, CHURCH OR EDUCATIONAL
GROUP (WITH CAPTIVE OR LIMITED
AUDIENCES SO THAT ADVERTISING
IS NOT NECESSARY...)

AND ANOTHER RACKET...

SUB-DISTRIBUTOR RENTS FILM TO ONE THEATER FOR WEEK 1, 2nd THEATER FOR WEEK 2, 3rd THEATER FOR WEEK 3.

ON FIRST THEATER	ON SECOND THEATER	ON THIRD THEATER

SUB-DISTRIBUTOR FORWARDS CONTRACT AND MONEY DUE TO EXHIBITOR	SUB-DISTRIBUTOR KEEPS CONTRACT A SECRET AND KEEPS ALL MONEY. HE TELLS DISTRIBUTOR THAT PRINT IS INACTIVE !	SUB-DISTRIBUTOR FORWARDS CONTRACT AND MONEY DUE TO EXHIBITOR

Step 1:

DISTRIBUTOR DISTRIBUTES A FILM FOR A PRODUCER. FILM HAS A GREAT BOX OFFICE POTENTIAL AND THE DISTRIBUTOR CAN GET TERMS OF 40% OF B.O. RECEIPTS.

Step 2:

DISTRIBUTOR ALSO HAS A SECOND FILM. BUT IT IS SO LOUSY THAT HE CAN'T PERSUADE EXHIBITORS TO PLAY IT FOR **FREE**!

Step 3:

SO... DISTRIBUTOR OFFERS THE 2 FILMS TO EXHIBITORS AS A PACKAGE (THE TERMS ARE 40% OF BOX OFFICE).

Step 4:

WHEN DISTRIBUTOR RECEIVES NET FILM RENTAL FROM EXHIBITOR, HE ALLOCATES ONE-HALF TO THE PRODUCER'S PICTURE, AND ONE-HALF TO THE BOMB!

(CONTINUED)

CHAPTER 35

RIGHT FINANCIAL TERMS

Suppose a picture has such little box office value that both the Exhibitor and the Distributor believe that the Exhibitor will not make his nut.

The Exhibitor may want the picture on 90/10. Under this plan, the entire box office up to the nut will go to the Exhibitor; if there is no excess above the nut, the Distributor will receive $0.

The Distributor may want to be paid a flat fee of $300. Under this plan the Distributor will receive $300.

The Right Financial Terms for the Exhibitor are 90/10; the Right Financial Terms for the Distributor are Flat Fee.

In fact, the Exhibitor might even want to 4 Wall the picture. That way the Exhibitor would receive his nut plus a profit; the Distributor would suffer a loss when box office receipts failed to be as high as the 4 Wall rental.

The big money, say some distributors, is made on percentage deals with exhibitors.

When a picture is fresh and highly publicized, the right deal may be a percentage deal. Later, the right deal may be a flat fee.

CHAPTER 36

RIGHT THEATRE

The distributor wants to receive the highest possible film rental; this does not mean that he will select the theatre with the highest box office potential.

For example, one big theatre may have a nut of $5,000 a week, while the small theatre across the street has a nut of $2,000 a week. Each theatre wants to play the film on a 90/10 arrangement. (Theatre receives the nut and 10% of any box office receipts above the nut.)

The distributor plans to allocate $1,000 of his advertising budget to the theatre which shows the film.

Let's examine the amount of Net Film Rental retained by the distributor under various circumstances.

	Big Theatre	Small Theatre
Box Office Receipts	$5,000	$5,000
— The Nut	— 5,000	— 2,000
	0	3,000
— Advertising	— 1,000	— 1,000
Loss to Distributor	— $1,000	
Excess Box Office		2,000
— 10% of Excess Box Office		— 200
90% of Excess Box Office		1,800
Net Film Rental		$1,800

BETTER THEATRE   SMALL THEATRE

In the just above case, the Right Theatre was the Small Theatre.

But one problem with Small Theatre is that it has only one-half of the seats of Big Theatre. If the picture is a big hit, then more people may want to see it than Small Theatre can accommodate.

Suppose 6,000 people wanted to pay $3 each to see the picture during a week. Big Theatre can seat 1,000 people at a time, and can accommodate all 6,000 during the 22 times the picture plays during the week. Small theatre has only 500 seats, and has to turn away 1,000 potential $3 ticket buyers.

	Big Theatre	Small Theatre
Box Office Receipts		
6000 x $3	$18,000	
5000 x $3		$15,000
— The Nut	5,000	2,000
	13,000	13,000
— Advertising	1,000	1,000
	12,000	12,000
— 10% of Excess Box Office		
	— 1,200	— 1,200
90% of Excess Box Office	10,800	10,800
Net Film Rental	$10,800	$10,800
BETTER THEATRE	SAME	SAME

Let's increase the potential ticket buyers to 10,000 people, which Big Theatre can seat. If these 10,000 tried to get into Little Theatre, only 6,000 would be seated.

	Big Theatre	Small Theatre
Box Office Receipts		
10,000 x $3	$30,000	
6,000 x $3		$18,000
— The Nut	5,000	2,000
	25,000	15,000
— Advertising	1,000	1,000
	24,000	14,000
— 10% of Excess Box Office	2,400	1,400
90% of Excess Box Office	21,600	12,600
Net Film Rental	$21,600	$12,600

BETTER THEATRE   BIG THEATRE

CHAPTER 37

ROUGH TERMS

When a Distributor has a hot film, a box office smash, he is in a better bargaining position then when he has a run-of-the-mill movie.

The Exhibitor wants to play the hit.

If the Exhibitor plays a different film each week, his playing a hit one week will benefit him not only that week but also the following week.

The Exhibitor wants to associate his theatre with pleasure in the public mind. The owner of the Bijoy can't afford to let the public think that all hits are played at the Broadway, and no hits are played at the Bijoy.

When a Distributor handles the initial release of a "SOUND OF MUSIC" a "GODFATHER," an "EXORCIST," a "DEEP THROAT," the Exhibitor may have to agree to rough terms.

1. **Front money.** The Exhibitor may have to pay a large advance to the Distributor.

2. **Extended playing time.** The Exhibitor may have to agree to play the film a certain minimum number of weeks.

3. **Weekly guarantee.** The Exhibitor may have to pay a weekly guarantee to the Distributor, whether or not the box office justifies the guarantee.

4. **Combination of the above.** For example, if an Exhibitor must pay a weekly guarantee of $4000 for a minimum playing time of 12 weeks, that sum is $48,000. The Exhibitor may be forced to pay half or all of the $48,000 months ahead of the play dates.

5. Minimum advertising costs. The Distributor may insist upon detailed and minimum advertising campaigns.

Sometimes, these and other rough terms are applied to a motion picture which shows great box office promise, but which becomes a box office disaster.

In such events, Exhibitors may suffer tremendous losses, and feel that they "have been had." Such feelings, rationalize some Exhibitors, justify everything Exhibitors do to "take" Distributors.

CHAPTER 38

RUNS

1. FIRST RUN in a geographic area. Theatre may be elegant showcase, a pleasure to visit, whatever may be playing. Financial terms may be NUT. 90—10. Distributor pays for advertising. Since all box office revenue comes only from one theatre, all advertising costs are allocated to that theatre. Generally only star-studded million plus dollar pictures can afford to gamble all advertising costs on box office receipts of one first run theatre.

2. MULTIPLE RUN in a geographic area. Several theatres which are wide enough apart to not compete for customers, but are close enough together to benefit from the major advertising expenses (commercials on television station(s) covering the area, advertisements in major newspapers covering the area) play the same picture(s) on the same dates. Thus, an advertising campaign which costs $12,000 can be spread among many theatres (8 theatres at $1500 each or 24 theatres at $500 each). The pictures can be million dollar productions, exploitation pictures, or any other kind which attracts large audiences.

3. RED CARPET THEATRES. Sometimes a picture may not be strong enough to be introduced in just one theatre, but it is deemed stronger at the box office than the ordinary pictures which come to a city on a multiple run. The picture may be given a RED CARPET THEATRE run by several theatres at the same time, followed by a multiple run in many theatres. This RED CARPET THEATRES treatment may be given to pictures with strong box office appeal to a limited audience which may be willing to travel to a RED CARPET THEATRE to see that picture (e.g., a British film, an art film, a widely publicized porno film).

4. SUBSEQUENT RUNS. There may still be an audience for a picture after its run in multiple locations

simultaneously. Some people may have missed the picture and want to see it. Other people don't travel out of their neighborhood to see a movie. The movie may still be useful as a second feature for which the distributor pays a flat fee.

5. The exhibitor who shows a motion picture wants protection against the picture being shown simultaneously in another competetive motion picture theatre. The exhibitor may want protection against the picture being shown elsewhere in the vicinity just before or just after the film is booked into his theatre. Or, the exhibitor may want to book the picture the day after it ends a prior run.

6. The Distributor-Exhibitor Contract discusses runs, territories, clearances.

CHAPTER 39

SCREENING ROOMS

Screening rooms can be found in studios, distributors and sub-distributors headquarters; there are also independently owned and operated screening rooms.

Some screening rooms have only 35mm projectors found in commercial theatres; other screening rooms also have 16mm projectors; other screening rooms have equipment which can play in sync a silent motion picture film and the not attached soundtrack.

Generally, screening rooms are comfortable, with comfortable chairs and sofas, available coffee; all in all, a setting ideal for making a buyer feel good and receptive to the film.

The buyer may be:
1. A distributor to whom the producer is trying to sell the concept of distributing the film.
2. Reporters and reviewers.
3. Exhibitors.
4. Sub-distributors and foreign distributors; television people.
5. Investors for future projects, or for some aspect of the film being exhibited.

PRODUCTION		PLAY DATES	TERMS	
NUMBER	TITLE		PERCENTAGE	NE

REMARKS:-

STATEMENT

GROSS		BILLED		PAID		BALANCE DUE	

CHAPTER 40

SLOW PAY / LOW PAY / NO PAY

The amount of money which an exhibitor is supposed to pay to the distributor can be computed by

(1) applying the terms of the Distributor—Exhibitor contract

(2) to the actual box office receipts.

Distributors and Exhibitors frequently play a game of treating the contractually owed amount as a mere starting point for further negotiations.

The Exhibitor states, "I did not gross as much money as I wanted to; therefore I am going to pay the Distributor less money than I promised to pay him."

By a fascinating custom of the industry, the power of the Exhibitor to breach the Distributor-Exhibitor contract is recognized.

The Exhibitor simply fails to pay anything to the Distributor until the Distributor agrees to settle for a lesser sum.

The Exhibitor thus (1) fails to pay on time, and becomes a slow-pay, (2) fails to pay the amount promised and becomes a low-pay, (3) may fail to pay at all, and becomes a no-pay.

One of the major distributors during the past half century was MGM. The exhibitors violated their contracts with MGM so often with this slow-pay, low-pay, no-pay technique, that MGM gave up its distribution business. (There were also other reasons for MGM's decision.)

This awesome power to break distributors and ruin producers is exercised in several ways.

For example, an Exhibitor-Distributor contract may call for advertising expenses to be shared. The Exhibitor is rather

slow in collecting (a) a tear sheet of each and every advertisement, (b) a correct bill for each and every advertisement. The
Exhibitor, after taking his sweet time, calculates the total
advertising expense and the percentages payable by the
Distributor and the Exhibitor.

If the Distributor disagrees with any item in the calculations, he may choose to dispute the item and thus give the
Exhibitor an excuse for holding up payment of the net film
rental as calculated by the Exhibitor.

One of the reasons Exhibitors hold up payments to
Distributors is the Exhibitors using the money to build new
theatres. New theatres mean the Exhibitor has more bargaining
power than ever before, and has more outlets in his area.

Chains are notorious for playing games of the delaying kind.
With their superior management, it is simple for chains to
swiftly calculate how much they owe distributors. But
individual managers of theatres belong to a chain may claim to
distributors that they have no authority to pay; payments are
made at headquarters. Unfortunately, many headquarters are
slow to pay.

CHAPTER 41

SUB-DISTRIBUTOR AGREEMENT

Agreement made between _____, a corporation incorporated in the State of California, hereinafter, for purposes of convenience, referred to as DISTRIBUTOR, and _____ , hereinafter for purposes of convenience, referred to as SUB-DISTRIBUTOR.

WITNESSETH

1.   DISTRIBUTOR hereby appoints SUB-DISTRIBUTOR as a sub-distributor in the Exchange Area or Territory consisting of:

_____

_____

(Definition of Exchange Area and environs are those covered by Major Film Distribution Companies.)
for the purpose of selling and distributing the motion picture(s) titled:

_____

_____

_____

2.   SUB-DISTRIBUTOR shall use only the contract forms approved by the DISTRIBUTOR: no contracts shall be effective for any purpose whatsoever unless first approved in writing by DISTRIBUTOR, and no agreements of any kind shall be made with theatres or exhibitors except in writing. No playdates shall be confirmed, or accepted, changed or modified without the mutual agreement of both parties hereto.

3.   SUB-DISTRIBUTOR shall be responsible for the liquidation of all contracts made by SUB-DISTRIBUTOR: meaning thereby that SUB-DISTRIBUTOR shall follow up all such contracts to the end that the same are completed in accordance with their terms; the picture played and all receipts due to DISTRIBUTOR received therefore. SUB-DISTRIBUTOR shall arrange for the receipt of all reports and film rentals due to the DISTRIBUTOR on all such approved contracts. It is the intention of the parties hereto, that SUB-DISTRIBUTOR be responsible for obtaining

payment and forwarding same forthwith to **DISTRIBUTOR**.

4. **SUB-DISTRIBUTOR** shall receive a commission of ____ %
on all revenue received on contracts that are entered into as a
result of the efforts of **SUB-DISTRIBUTOR**, or made in the
territory described above, (other than certain key theatres or
situations established by the Home Office or Circuit deals
booked by the Home Office as may hereinafter be specified in
writing). **SUB-DISTRIBUTOR** will receive one half of commission established for these bookings. **SUB-DISTRIBUTOR** will
mail a photostat copy of check(s) received from exhibitor for
film rental and a **SUB-DISTRIBUTOR'S** check, less commission
due **SUB-DISTRIBUTOR** to be mailed to **DISTRIBUTOR once
a week** with our **BILLING & COLLECTION REPORT**, all
collections to be listed per instructions on **COLLECTION
REPORT**. If "no collections," report must be sent to
DISTRIBUTOR weekly with a notation "no collections this
week." Above to be mailed to **DISTRIBUTOR** at _____
_____ .

5. All remuneration of any kind or nature whatsoever
received, or to be received, under and pursuant to said approved
contract, shall be made payable to **SUB-DISTRIBUTOR** by
Exhibitor and shall be, immediately upon receipt by **SUB—
DISTRIBUTOR**, forwarded to the office of **DISTRIBUTOR** at
_____ .

6. **DISTRIBUTOR** agrees to furnish to **SUB-DISTRIBUTOR**
sufficient prints to properly service all of the accounts having
properly approved contracts and play dates.

7. It shall be the responsibility of **SUB-DISTRIBUTOR** to see
to it that all prints are exhibited without any change of any
nature whatsoever, including credits. All such prints shall remain
the sole property of **DISTRIBUTOR**, and shall be returned by
SUB-DISTRIBUTOR in the same condition as when received, it
being the understanding of the parties hereto that **SUB-
DISTRIBUTOR** shall be responsible for any damage or loss
occasioned thereto while in the possession of **SUB-DISTRIBUTOR**
or the Exhibitor. **SUB-DISTRIBUTOR** hereby undertakes to
insure **DISTRIBUTOR'S** prints against loss or damage at
prevailing laboratory replacement costs.

8.   SUB-DISTRIBUTOR agrees to furnish DISTRIBUTOR on request, a list of all existing contracts; theatres or exhibitors with whom negotiations are pending for the execution of such contracts; advance play dates or bookings, and any other information required by DISTRIBUTOR. SUB-DISTRIBUTOR agrees to maintain complete and detailed records showing all contracts executed; bookings; exhibition and performance results; box office reports and collections, and agrees to make same available to DISTRIBUTOR or its authorized representative to inspect and audit the same.

9.   Shipping charges from DISTRIBUTOR to SUB-DISTRIBUTOR shall be paid for by DISTRIBUTOR. Shipping and/or transportation charges for prints between SUB-DISTRIBUTOR and exhibitor shall be paid by SUB-DISTRIBUTOR or by the theatre.

10.   Should SUB-DISTRIBUTOR encounter any undue difficulties in securing payment from a delinquent account or accounts, SUB-DISTRIBUTOR is authorized to take legal action, if necessary, at DISTRIBUTOR'S cost.
     SUB-DISTRIBUTOR also has DISTRIBUTOR'S approval to send delinquent account or accounts (beyond 45 days) a statement charging _____ monthly interest for outstanding balances.

11.   This agreement shall terminate _____ years from and after the date hereof without further notice by either party. However, the within contract may be cancelled on thirty (30) days written notice by either party. In the event of such cancellation, all approved contracts shall be honored by both parties hereto, meaning thereby that SUB-DISTRIBUTOR shall continue to be responsible for the liquidation of all approved contracts; DISTRIBUTOR shall be obliged to pay to SUB-DISTRIBUTOR the appropriate commission on same, and DISTRIBUTOR shall be obliged to provide the appropriate prints and other articles to be provided in accordance herewith.

12.   In the event of any dispute arising out of the execution of the within contract, or the breach thereof by either party hereto, and the institution of litigation, it is agreed that the prevailing party in any such litigation shall be entitled to recover all damages sustained by it, plus a reasonable attorney's fee.

All arbitration shall be in the State of California.

Executed at Los Angeles, California, this _____ day of
——————— , 197 ——.

DISTRIBUTOR

By ————————————————————————

SUB-DISTRIBUTOR

By ————————————————————————

CHAPTER 42

THEATRE EXPENSES

One of the possible financial arrangements between Distributor and Exhibitor is the "4 wall arrangement." The Exhibitor is paid a flat fee by the Distributor for the rental of the theatre and its personnel for the rental period.

The amount paid by a Distributor depends on several factors. One factor known to the Exhibitor is his cost of operating the theatre. The Exhibitor will normally want to receive at least the cost of operation plus a profit.

Theatre expenses include, but are not limited to:

1. Manager
2. Assistant Manager(s)
3. Doormen.
4. Cashiers.
5. Usher(s).
6. Projectionist(s).
7. Candy counter person(s).
8. Parking attendant(s).
9. Janitor(s).
10. Bookkeeper.
11. Maintenance and repair of projection room equipment, screen.
12. Maintenance and repair of theatre, seats, lobby, lobby display.
13. Advertising, institutional.
14. Advertising for specific pictures.
15. Marque changing service.
16. Print pick-up and delivery service.
17. Tickets.
18. Report envelopes and forms.
19. Office supplies and stamps.
20. House supplies, bulbs.
21. Uniforms and cleaning.

22. Coat room attendant(s), hangers, tickets.
23. Depreciation of equipment and screen, seats, carpets, etc.
24. Depreciation of building.
25. Rent of theatre.
26. Equipment rentals.
27. Services — Legal
28. Services — Accounting and Bookkeeping.
29. Services — Cleaning nightly, weekly, annually.
30. Services — Secretarial.
31. Taxes — U.S. Withholding Tax — Income.
32. Taxes — State Withholding Tax — Income.
33. Taxes — U.S. Social Security Tax Withheld from Employees.
34. Taxes — U.S. Social Security Tax — Employers Share.
35. Taxes — State Unemployment Tax or Disability Tax Withheld from Employees.
36. Taxes — State Unemployment Tax or Disability Tax Employers Share.
37. Licenses — County, City, Local.
38. Real property and personal property taxes.
39. Insurance(s).
40. Other.

CHAPTER 43

THREE ACTIVITIES

1. The glamorous activity   —   PRODUCTION

2. The unknown activity   —   DISTRIBUTION

3. The public activity   —   EXHIBITION

FLOW OF MONEY

1. CUSTOMER pays EXHIBITOR

2. EXHIBITOR pays many expenses
   EXHIBITOR may pay DISTRIBUTOR

3. DISTRIBUTOR pays many expenses
   DISTRIBUTOR may pay PRODUCER's debts.
   DISTRIBUTOR may pay PRODUCER.

4. PRODUCER may pay expenses
   PRODUCER may repay loans
   PRODUCER may pay backers
   PRODUCER may have a profit.

CHAPTER 44

TICKETS

Contracts with Exhibitors may have provisions concerning the tickets.

1. Every admission must be by a ticket sold by a cashier.

2. The cashier will issue a "Pass" ticket to each passholder, who must surrender each one-time pass to the cashier. The cashier shall have all continual pass holders sign a register before issuing him a "Pass ticket."

3. All tickets must be consecutively numbered, and sold consecutively.

4. The customer shall give his ticket to a doorman, who shall tear the ticket in two halves (a) horizontally, or (b) vertically.

5. The ticket taker shall throw the half-ticket which he retains in the proper slot of the ticket box. There shall be a separate slot for each type of ticket.

6. Each hour (or each time prices change) the ticket box shall be emptied into envelopes which identify the type of ticket, the date, the time period covered, the numbers of the first and last tickets.

7. The cashier shall also keep records hourly, when prices change, each time the cashier enters or leaves the booth, concerning the type of ticket, the date, the time period covered, the numbers of the first and last tickets.

8. The manager shall double-check the reports of the cashier and the door-man.

9. The manager shall calculate the amount of money which the cashier should have for sale of tickets.

10. The cashier shall count the money in the box office; the manager shall count the money, too.

11. Tickets representing different amounts shall be in different colors.

12. The door-man and cashier must be discouraged from personal private enterprise games. In one such game the cashier sells tickets from her own privately printed roll; the door-man keeps the ticket; the two split the proceeds. A second game has the cashier sell proper tickets; the door-man obtains the tickets from the customers; the door-man returns the tickets to the cashier; the cashier resells the same tickets; the two split the proceeds from one set of sales and the theatre receives the proceeds from the other set of sales.

13. Tickets are proof of their purchase and the right to be in the theatre. Customers should be encouraged to hold on to tickets, so that persons, who are suspected of sneaking in, cannot pick up thrown away tickets.

14. Ticket numbers and prices are indicated on daily reports and weekly reports. Reports often require hourly information for each type of tickets.

15. Managers should count the house each hour and irregularly, and write such information on forms. This count may be inconsistent with reported ticket sales. If so, the inconsistency should be investigated.

CHAPTER 45

USABLE, INCORRECT RATIOS

1. PUBLIC pay EXHIBITOR one box office dollar. 100%

2. EXHIBITOR pays overhead and makes profit. 40%
   EXHIBITOR pays local advertising expenses
     for himself and distributor 20%
   EXHIBITOR pays DISTRIBUTOR "Net Film
     Rental" 40%

3. DISTRIBUTOR pays SUB-DISTRIBUTOR 10%
   DISTRIBUTOR pays overhead & makes profit 10%
   DISTRIBUTOR pays freight & national adver-
     tising and prints 10%
   DISTRIBUTOR allocates to PRODUCER 10%

(Please note that in this case 10% of BOX OFFICE DOLLAR
equals 25% of NET FILM RENTAL.)

4. DISTRIBUTOR—PRODUCER contract may provide that
   DISTRIBUTOR re-pays PRODUCTION items:
       DISTRIBUTOR repays PRODUCER's bank loans
       DISTRIBUTOR pays PRODUCER's creditors
       DISTRIBUTOR pays PRODUCER's deferrals
       DISTRIBUTOR pays PRODUCER's profit participants
       DISTRIBUTOR pays PRODUCER.

5. PRODUCER pays overhead.
   PRODUCER pays backers.
   PRODUCER keeps profit.

   Percentages vary from picture to picture. For example,
some distributors may receive more less than the 25% + 25% of
NET FILM RENTAL allocated to the DISTRIBUTOR and the
SUB-DISTRIBUTOR in the above example.

WEEKLY SHIPPING SHEET

INSTITUTE FOR ADULT EDUCATION
P.O. BOX 2710, HOLLYWOOD, CALIFORNIA 90028

DATE _____

SHIPMENTS FOR WEEK _____ DATE FROM _____ TO _____ BRANCH _____

LINE NO.	THEATRE	TOWN	ST.	PLAYDATES	FEATURE NUMBER	FEATURE TITLE	NO. OF REELS	SHIP VIA	DATE DUE BACK

BOOKER _____

RETURN ORIGINAL AND ONE COPY TO INSTITUTE FOR ADULT EDUCATION

FORM 9

-148-

BIBLIOGRAPHY

ACTION is the magazine of the Directors Guild of America, 7950 Sunset Boulevard, Hollywood, CA 90046. Excellent publication which contains articles concerning directors. Distributors distributing pictures with "stars" who don't have box office value may wish to publicize the director or other pictures of the same genre. Book reviews.

AMERICAN CINEMATOGRAPHER, 1782 North Orange Drive, Hollywood, CA 90028. Excellent publication which emphasizes the cinematographers' contribution to films. Articles may supply usable quotes for advertising to consumers. Distributors may encourage publicists to contribute articles for pictures being distributed. Film reviews, book reviews. New equipment. Distributors occasionally publicize technique or equipment to promote public curiosity. Sometimes publicized cinematographers are part of the package used to promote money.

BACK STAGE is a trade publication, 165 West 46th Street, New York City 10036. Features include news, advertisements, book reviews, casting information (this feature can provide independent distributors with information about independent pictures which may need distribution).

BOX OFFICE is a trade publication, 825 Van Brunt Blvd., Kansas City, MO 64124. Key aids to distributors include advertisements with claimed box office figures, Box Office Barometer, Feature Reviews, Feature Chart, Box Office Booking Guide, Review Digest.

BULLETIN published by Academy of Motion Picture Arts and Sciences, 9038 Melrose Avenue, Hollywood, CA 90069.

CLASSIC FILM COLLECTOR is a trade and fun publication in the 8mm and 16mm fields. Producers and distributors who want to acquire prints of old pictures (possibly with a view of making a modern re-make) can benefit from the editorial and advertising content. 734 Philadelphia Street, Indiana, PA 15701.

DAILY VARIETY is a trade publication. 1400 North Cahuenga Boulevard, Hollywood, CA 90028. Key aids to distributors include news concerning anticipated productions, completed productions, box office figures in New York and Los Angeles, movie reviews, advertisements, stock market charts and other financial information.

ENTERTAINMENT PUBLISHING AND THE ARTS : AGREEMENTS AND THE LAW (1963, 1969) Clark Boardman, New York.

FILMMAKERS NEWSLETTER (The Magazine For Creative Filmmakers). P.O. Box 482, Marblehead, Mass. 01945. Excellent publication which should be collected and bound annually. Distributors who want to distribute films which are entertaining and different should read, and have their prospective producers read this publication regularly.

FILM INDUSTRIES (Practical Business/Legal Problems in Production, Distribution, and Exhibition) by Michael F. Mayer (1973) Hastings House, New York.

FILM SUPERLIST: 20,000 MOTION PICTURES IN THE U.S. PUBLIC DOMAIN by Johnny Minus and William Storm Hale (1973) Seven Arts Press, Inc., 6605 Hollywood Boulevard, Hollywood, CA 90028. $95.00. Over 56,000 films of 1894-1939 are listed. Those still protected by copyright because the copyright was renewed are identified. The pictures which were not subject of a copyright renewal registration are identified. An article discusses public domain.

FILM ·TV LAW (Your Introduction To Film · TV Copyright, Contracts and Other Law) by Johnny Minus and William Storm Hale (1973) Seven Arts Press, Inc., 6605 Hollywood Boulevard, Hollywood, CA 90028. $10.00. Excellent introduction for film students and professionals in the easy to read illustrated text, which contains sample forms and contracts. Is used as classroom text in film school.

HOLLYWOOD REPORTER is a trade publication. 6715 Sunset Boulevard, Hollywood, CA 90028. Key aids to distributors include announcements concerning proposed productions, Feature Production chart, film reviews, advertisements, book reviews, trade news.

HOW TO INVEST IN MOTION PICTURES . . . AND WHY YOU SHOULDN'T by Tom Laughlin (1971) Taylor-Laughlin Investment Corp., Los Angeles.

INDEPENDENT FILM JOURNAL is a trade publication. 1251 Avenue of the Americas, New York, NY 10020. Its editorials discuss distributor-exhibitor conflicts. Advertisements mention claimed box office grosses. Booking information includes reviews, distributor and film releasing news. Its coverage of litigation and legislation concerning censorship and obscenity is excellent.

INTERNATIONAL FILM GUIDE. Annual A.S. Barnes & Co., South Brunswick & N.Y. The Tantivy Press. 108 New Bond Street, London WIYOQX. Articles, advertisements, copy concerning new films, screening rooms, equipment, theatres, etc. Distributors thinking of distributing foreign films need this publication.

INTERNATIONAL MOTION PICTURE ALMANAC. Annual. Quigley Publishing Company, New York. Essential publication each year. Who's who and done what. Older issues are useful in indicating whether current companies are recent or older (established). Lists of drive-ins, equipment, services. World market.

LAW OF FREIGHT LOSS AND DAMAGE CLAIMS. Richard R. Sigman. Wm. C. Brown Company Publishers, Dubuque, Iowa, 1967.

LAW OF THE STAGE, SCREEN AND RADIO by Roger Marchete, (1936) Suttonhouse Limited, San Francisco, Los Angeles, New York.

LEGAL AND BUSINESS PROBLEMS OF MOTION PICTURE INDUSTRY, edited by Paul A. Baumgarten (1973) Practicing Law Institute, New York.

LIVELIEST ART by Arthur Knight, Mentor Books, New American Library, New York, 1959.

MANAGERS, ENTERTAINERS & AGENTS BOOK by Johnny Minus and William Storm Hale (1971) Seven Arts Press, Inc., Hollywood, CA 90028. $35.00.

MOTION PICTURE THEATER MANAGEMENT by Harold B. Franklin, George H. Doran Company, 1927.

MOVIE INDUSTRY:AMERICAN FILM INDUSTRY PRACTICE by A. William Bluem (1972) Hastings House, N.Y.

MOVIE INDUSTRY BOOK by Johnny Minus and William Storm Hale (1970, 1974). Seven Arts Press, Inc. 6605 Hollywood Boulevard, Hollywood, CA 90028. $35.00. Essential book for film lawyer, producer, film student. Parts on 1. Putting A Picture Together, 4. Partnerships, 5. Distribution Practices, 7. Laboratory Agreement, 8. Producer-Distributor Agreement, 9. Copyright, 11. Long Contracts, 12. Short Forms and Contracts, 14. Budgets.

MUSIC INDUSTRY BOOK by Walter E. Hurst and William Storm Hale (1963, 1974). Seven Arts Press, Inc., Hollywood, CA 90028. $25.00.

OBSCENITY AND THE LAW Course Handbook. Practicing Law Institute, 1133 Avenue of The Americas, New York, NY 10036. $20.00. 1974.

PERFORMING ARTS MANAGEMENT AND LAW by Joseph Taubman. (1972-73) Forms. Law-Arts Publishing, New York.

PRODUCING, FINANCING AND DISTRIBUTING FILM by
Paul A. Baumgarten and Donald C. Farber (1973) Drama
Book Specialists, New York.

PUBLISHERS OFFICE MANUAL (How To Do Paperwork In
The Music Publishing Industry) by Walter E. Hurst and William
Storm Hale. (1966, 1974). Seven Arts Press, Inc. Hollywood,
CA 90028. $25.00.

RECORD INDUSTRY BOOK by Walter E. Hurst and William
Storm Hale. (1961, 1974). Seven Arts Press, Inc. Hollywood,
CA 90028. $25.00.

SYLLABUS AND FORMS ON NON-STUDIO AND OTHER
NOVEL SOURCES AND METHODS OF FINANCING
MOTION PICTURES (1974) Beverly Hills Bar Association,
Beverly Hills, and University of Southern California Law
Center, Los Angeles.

TOTAL FILM-MAKER by Jerry Lewis (1971) Random House,
New York.

U.S. MASTER PRODUCERS AND BRITISH MUSIC SCENE
BOOK by Walter E. Hurst and William Storm Hale (1966,
1974). Seven Arts Press, Inc. Hollywood, CA 90028. $25.00.

VARIETY (Weekly) is a trade publication. 154 West 46th
Street, NY 10036. It is a weekly, and benefits by having the
scope that longer preparation time provides and that being
able to extract stories and reviews from Daily Variety
furnishes. Lots of U.S. and foreign reviews, news, and
advertisements. Lots of box office information from all over
the United States. Charts of top weekly, annual, and historical
money makers.

GLOSSARY

A.F.A.A. — Adult Film Association of America.

A.F.I. — American Film Institute.

BLIND SELLING is a term often applied to a system of block booking defined as the leasing of a number or group of pictures, the subject, titles or time of availability of which are not known when the contract is made.

BLOCK BOOKING is a plan whereby films are offered in blocks; a block is a group of films offered as a unit containing a number of individual motion pictures which are available for lease by exhibitors for stated periods (e.g., 3 months to several years).

CATEGORY OF FILMS
X — Children are not admitted regardless of parents' wishes. No one under 17 admitted.
R — Restricted: under 17 requires accompanying parent or adult guardian.
G — General audiences: all ages are admitted.
PG— Parental guidance suggested.
C — "Condemned" by National Catholic Film Office.

CLEARANCE is a restraint, a provision in the distributor-exhibitor agreement to the effect that the picture will not be licensed for exhibition by a competing exhibitor for a stated period of time subsequent to the completion of the prior exhibitor's run.

COOPERATIVE ADVERTISING: The distributor and the exhibitor each pay a percentage of advertising costs; often the percentage of contribution of advertising is the same as the percentage of sharing box office gross receipts.

ILLEGAL PRACTICES include 1. fixing of admission prices by the distributor, 2. unreasonable clearances, 3. conditioning of a license for one motion picture upon the acceptance of a license for another.

MPAA RATINGS — G, PG, R, X.

MULTIPLE RUN — exhibiting a film in many theatres in a locality at the same time.

N.A.C. — National Association of Concessionaires.

90—10 DEAL — the distributor receives 90% of the gross box office receipts after the exhibitor deducts a house allowance figure.

NODL — National Organization for Decent Literature.

S.M.P.T.E. — Society of Motion Picture And Television Engineers.

"STAGGERED RUNS" is a method of distribution in which pictures are licensed for first exhibition at the larger theatres or those able to return a larger film rental and will subsequently be licensed in stages to other theatres which return lesser film rentals.

T.E.A. — Theatre Equipment Association.

INDEX